Harriett Ellison
Rt 3 Box 158
Culpeper, Va 22701
703-547 2022

THE ADVENTURES OF HEALING

by

Pastor Donald W. Bartow

Life Enrichment Publishers
P.O. Box 526
Canton, Ohio 44701

Acknowledgements

What an Adventure this book has been. However, like every other journey it has not been made alone. It would have been impossible without a host of friends and helpers.

I want to acknowledge my indebtedness to my good friend, Clair B. King, M.D. He, in a sense, is my spiritual father in the area of Spiritual Healing. His influence in my life cannot be measured. This book started with the encouragement he gave to me many years ago. I will always be grateful for what he and his dear wife Marion have meant to me and our family.

My wife, Mary, and our children Dennis and Beckie and their families have been a source of encouragement through the years. They all have been used of God to inspire and undergird me in my efforts.

The members and friends of Westminster Church have been a source of inspiration to me. These dear friends have provided me with the prayer support and spiritual encouragement to write in the midst of the duties and demands of being a parish pastor.

There are many throughout the nation who have encouraged me to put in writing what I seek to proclaim in my preaching. Too numerous to mention, yet too important to neglect, I acknowledge the contribution these individuals have made toward the writing of this book.

In short, I simply happen to be the one who has brought together the efforts of hundreds. The book has not been written by me, but by all who have contributed in any way to it. I thank God for each and give to Him the glory.

DWB

The Adventures

Scripture portions printed in this book are from the *King James Version* unless otherwise indicated.

ISBN 0-938736-19-1 (paper)
ISBN 0-938736-21-3 (cloth)
LCCN 80-84933

What is Spiritual Healing

What is a meaningful and workable definition of Spiritual Healing? How should a person look at a reasonable approach for the church and healing? These and many other questions arise when considering healing.

A DEFINITION

Spiritual Healing is wholeness. It is the healing of the whole person. It is soundness of body, mind and spirit.

CHANNELS

The channels for Spiritual Healing include prayer, laying-on-of-hands, anointing with oil, confession, the sacraments, etc. All of these things become significant by the power of the Holy Spirit in response to faith in God through Jesus Christ.

NO SUBSTITUTE FOR MEDICINE

Although it may result in physical healings, Spiritual Healing is not a substitute for medicine or surgery. It makes no claims to prescribe in the areas of medicine, surgery, psychiatry, and psychology. It works closely with all involved in these allied professions dedicated to healing. Members of the allied professions of healing realize and appreciate the great value of faith in the healing process. All healing is of God. Individuals are but His instruments regardless of their profession in the area of healing.

THEOLOGICALLY SOUND

Spiritual Healing is theologically sound and is in harmony with:

1. Orthodox Christian theology,
2. The teaching and life-style of Jesus Christ, and
3. The practice of the Apostolic Church.

It is an obedient response to the Divine Commission given by Jesus to *"go preach and heal."*

BASED ON GOD'S LAWS

Spiritual Healing is not magic, sleight of hand, or hocus pocus. It is based on God's laws of faith and love just as medical healing is based on God's physical laws. The many miracles of Spiritual Healing do not break natural laws, but are the result of higher laws which many times we do not understand.

THE TERM SPIRITUAL HEALING

Spiritual Healing is sometimes called Christian Healing because it comes from Christ and its meaning and its ends are Christian.

Some refer to it as Faith Healing. This term falls short because often there is no clear understanding in whom faith is placed. This is not always made plain by some so-called *"faith healers."*

Spiritual Healing has by some been called Divine Healing. This is too broad of a term because, in a sense, all healing is divine.

Spiritual Healing differs from Christian Science as it acknowledges the reality of pain, disease, and evil.

A SANE, SENSIBLE APPROACH

The Church's healing ministry has often been in disrepute because of abuses by charlatans and those seeking their own gain. These individuals and experiences are deeply regretted, but are not the criteria to determine the validity of Spiritual Healing

Perhaps the major Protestant Churches have frowned on the healing ministry because of emotional excesses, the extreme theological views of some, and the over-emphasis upon physical healing to the neglect of the spirit.

However, today an approach to healing is developing which is thoroughly based upon Christian concepts and acceptable to leaders of all major denominations.

WIDELY ACCEPTED TODAY

Hundreds of congregations now conduct regular Spiritual Healing services. Each month many others begin this adventure of faith.

I conducted my first public service of healing in May 1959. The years have added excitement to my effort to proclaim the wholeness the Lord has for each of us.

It has been my pleasant experience to discover that the practice of Spiritual Healing has three main benefits. It inspires individuals to greater devotion, leads them to richer experiences in worship, and deepens their understanding of the Bible.

The Goal of Spiritual Healing

It would be great if I could convey to all that the GOAL of Spiritual Healing is Jesus Christ. There are far too many who feel that a physical healing is the chief aim of the healing ministry. Nothing could be further from the truth.

KNOWING THE GREAT PHYSICIAN

The true GOAL of Spiritual Healing is knowing the Great Physician and not simply being healed by Him. Jesus never did say that you must be physically perfect, but He did say that you *"must be born again."* John 3:7. It is only through the spirit that you can discern the things of the spirit. See I Cor. 1:10-14.

It is a thrill to see individuals healed in body and emotions. However, it is a greater thrill to see them come to personally know the One who is the Great Physician. It is great for you to receive His gifts, but even more important that you receive Him who is the greatest gift.

ACCEPTING CHRIST

A letter from my good friend the Reverend Peter McFarland sums up the essence of Spiritual Healing. He had attended one of our Clergy-Lay Conferences on Healing and this influenced his actions concerning the incidents discussed in his letter as follows:

> *"In the light of the Conference on Spiritual Healing I preached a sermon on the Healing Power of Christ. One couple was in church who average about one Sunday a month in church. The Friday after they heard that sermon their eight-year-old son was hit by a car while riding his mini bike on the highway. The boy was unconscious in the hospital, so I went in and had prayer and laying on of hands for him with his parents. The boy regained consciousness Monday night, and has improved steadily ever since. Needless to say, the parents went through quite an emotional experience. The father, who did not join the church when the rest of the family did, vowed with his wife in the hospital to accept Jesus Christ."*

The little boy received a healing, but the father received an even more wonderful healing.

I feel Edward Winckley gets to the heart of the matter in the article appearing on page 18 of the April-June issue of the WORLD HEALING DIGEST.

> *"He for whom the martyrs died is He by whom we must live. That is what Christianity is and almost nothing else at all. That main, if not the sole, purpose of Healing Evangelism is to give people a supreme opportunity of encountering Jesus Christ and of binding themselves ever more closely to Him through faith. We must be desperately serious in this. Spiritual Healing means more than physical cure by spiritual aids. It is the outcome of union with God in Christ Jesus the Healer.*
>
> *So the creed of the believer in Spiritual Healing today is Jesus Christ as Healer. Not primarily being well or doing good, not good health or even good behavior, but God Himself in focus in Jesus Christ. We do not teach sufferers to believe in healing, but in Jesus Christ. The believer in Spiritual Healing is therefore never disappointed, because he is seeking, not things, but God. Christianity for the first disciples was not primarily a matter of behavior, but of belief. They believed that Christ was of God and that He believed in them. What could be more exciting than that? They did not discuss or hold conferences about Spiritual Healing; they preached and healed. When we believe what they believed we achieve in miracles of healing what they received. They practiced Healing Evangelism and 'turned the world upside-down.' We can do the same."*

I believe that many people today are saying as the Greeks of old, *"we would see Jesus."* (John 12:21)

All efforts of the ministry of healing should be expended to lead individuals to Jesus. It is He you need. May you accept Him now and in His fullness.

Why a Spiritual Healing Service

I said the following years ago and I still believe it. *"If I were the only one willing to be present, I would still hold a regular Spiritual Healing Service. It is a source of strength to me and a worthwhile discipline in my life."*

THE HUB

I know that a public Spiritual Healing Service is the hub of any strong emphasis in this area. It is the visible channel through which the local church says to its entire membership and to the community that God is in the healing business.

Some will say, *"Should not every worship service be a healing service and thus what is the need of a special one?"* This is a good question. However, we all know that the average worship service is not one in which individuals are made aware of God's healing power.

All aspects of our Christian Faith should be a part of every worship service. Yet, congregations have special times for evangelism, missions, stewardship, etc. We need this special emphasis for us to know and to remain aware of our church's ministry to individuals.

A public service of healing will enable a congregation to more adequately say:

I. GOD WILLS WHOLENESS

You can categorically believe the Lord wills wholeness. He even made your body to ingenuously combat disease. The very forces of nature cry for your wholeness.

Jesus did not hesitate to heal the sick. He demonstrated again and again that the heavenly Father desires wholeness for His children.

The promises of scripture confirm the Lord's desire for your wholeness. They are promises upon which we can base our hope for our healing.

II. MAN — UNITY

An individual cannot be considered as a being having a separate mind, separate body, separate spirit.

These three are not independent entities. They cannot be dealt with in isolation.

What you think influences how your body feels.

In like manner the tone of your spiritual health determines the state of your emotional and mental outlook.

How you feel physically will even affect your spiritual vitality. You are a unity and must be treated and considered in this light.

III. WHOLENESS INVOLVES ALL THINGS

You are affected by all of your relationships. Your attitude toward other people and the world about you deeply influences your well-being.

The attitudes and relationships with others must also be a part of the foci of wholeness in your life. There is more to you than your own mind, body, and spirit.

The message of Spiritual Healing is more than simply, *"Lord, heal me!"* It is the realization that all aspects of life need the healing touch of the Lord.

IV. POSITIVE POWER AVAILABLE

The positive, healing, reconciling, God-provided spiritual forces are available to you. They can especially be channeled into areas of your needs through the presence and prayers of God's people.

Indeed, prayer is better understood as a focusing of spiritual power than the verbalizing of one's requests unto the Almightly.

I implore you to permit every aspect of your life to be open to the powerful presence of the Lord. There is no aspect too small or too large for the Lord to consider.

V. ATTEND A HEALING SERVICE

This fifth point is obvious if you agree with the above four. You should put forth effort to attend a healing service.

If your church has no healing service, why not begin to pray and work toward starting one? In the meantime, perhaps you can attend one in a nearby church.

I present the above reasons for a healing service. I can't think of any reason not to have or

When to Begin a Healing Service

Often I am asked, *"When should a congregation begin conducting healing services?"* I answer this question on pages 198-200 of my book, *"Creative Churchmanship."* A summary follows:

ARE YOU WILLING

The basic question is, are you willing to start. If you are a pastor, dare to lead your people. If you are a lay person, dare to challenge your pastor, and together go forward in the healing ministry.

NO PERFECT TIME

It can be debated at length whether or not the time is right for the local congregation to begin conducting a public healing service. There is no perfect and complete answer to this problem. I have been privileged to speak to clergy and laity in many denominations regarding the blessings, pitfalls, and mechanics of the healing ministry. The preponderance of them have reacted with, *"Our people are not quite ready for this."*

To our shame, although the Church has existed for nearly two thousand years, most congregations are not quite ready in many areas — complete stewardship commitment, a sensible program of evangelism, worship services that speak to the heart, or public healing services.

NEVER WILL ALL AGREE

I do not want to say that every congregation should plunge blindly into a program of a public healing ministry. I cannot answer for a particular congregation; but I can say that, in some instances, ten years from now will be no different — that is, some churches will still be discussing, investigating, studying, praying for guidance, attending seminars and conferences to decide whether or not there should be a public healing service in their local church.

If lay people and pastors wait until everyone in their church is convinced of the validity of the healing ministry, they will never start.

This is illustrated by the fact that if any church waited until all its members showed up at a Sunday morning worship service, they would never open the doors. If they waited until only half their members showed up, few churches would experience corporate worship on any given Sunday, including Easter. If Paul had waited until all the pagans pleaded for the power of the Gospel in their lives, he never would have proclaimed the riches of the Redeemer.

LEARN AS YOU GO

Much time can be spent laying the foundation for an event and then moving forward from the findings. There is the other side of the coin — where the event takes place and you learn as you go along. In most churches, the latter approach is the best.

It is simply true that, when something happens, you learn! How many would be married, and have children, if they were required to have know all about it before the event took place? I took child psychology in college, but, believe me, you can't put in a book what God puts in a little life. I knew some of the aspects of personality development, but I learned a great deal more the first week after a little girl blessed our home. I have learned more from her than I did studying psychology and writing term papers concerning child development.

EXPERIENCE — EDUCATION

This is not to minimize education, but simply to say that education without experience leads only to untried book knowledge.

Experience without education and instruction leads only to feelings without adequate foundation. Christian creativity blends experience with education; education with experience.

As long as we say we are not quite ready, we can never be blamed for failing. As long as a person is in preparation, he cannot be held responsible for what he is not doing.

In a spirit of prayer, unity, and dedication, the congregation should seek to go forward in the Spirit of the Lord.

TRUST THE LORD

No pastor or layperson can claim to know all about God and His ways. At the same time you cannot say you are really trusting the Lord until you have made a venture of faith, and discovered the joy of adventures beyond yourself as found in Christ.

LOOK TO JESUS

We know not the end of what we begin, but we know Him who is the beginning and the end.

We know not what blessings He has in store, but we know He has many blessings to bestow upon us.

We know not what opposition we shall encounter, but we know what inner strength we have found.

We do not choose to look back and become a pillar of salt, but to look ahead and to be the salt of the earth.

Thus, looking unto Jesus, the Author and Finisher of our Faith, we worship, praise, and trust Him.

The big secret is to get-going for the Lord. Now!

Some Old Testament Miracles

It is practically impossible to list all of the miracles contained in the Old Testament. There are the interpretation of dreams, the appearances of the Angel of the Lord, revelations of coming events, special victories over Israel's enemies, fire falling upon the altar, etc. However, I do want to list some of the most outstanding ones. You may desire to carefully consider each scripture reference. It is obvious that the power of the Lord was revealed to many individuals throughout the ages.

I. MIRACLES IN THE BOOK OF GENESIS

1. Creation — Genesis Chapter 1
2. Enoch's translation — Genesis 5:24
3. The flood — Genesis Chapters 6-8
4. Sodom & Gomorroh destroyed — Genesis 19:15-29

II. MIRACLES IN THE TIME OF MOSES & JOSHUA

5. The burning bush — Ex. 3:1-4
6. The rod a serpent — Ex. 4:1-5
7. The leprous hand — Ex. 4:6-8
8. Nile water to blood — Ex. 4:9-12
9. Rod a serpent — Ex. 7:8-13
10. Water into blood — Ex. 7:14-24
11. Plague of frogs — Ex. 8:1-15
12. Plague of lice — Ex. 8:16-19
13. Plague of flies — Ex. 8:20-32
14. Plagues of death of cattle and of boils — Ex. 9:1-12
15. Plague of hail and fire — Ex. 9:13-35
16. Plague of locusts — Ex. 10:1-20
17. Plague of three days of darkness — Ex. 10:21-29
18. Death of first born — Ex. 11:1-10; 12:29-36
19. Pillar of cloud and fire — Ex. 13:21,22
20. Crossing of Red Sea — Ex. 14
21. Marah water healed — Ex. 15:23-26
22. Manna given — Ex. 16:14-36; Num. 11:7-9
23. Quails given — Ex. 16:12,13; Num. 11:18-34
24. Water from the rock — Ex. 17:1-7
25. Water from another rock — Num. 20:1-13
26. Kept 40 days on mount — Ex. 24:18
27. Kept again 40 days on mount — Ex. 34:28
28. Moses face shining — Ex. 34:29-35
29. Miriam's leprosy — Num. 12:10-15
30. Earth's opening — Num. 16:29-34
31. Fire from the Lord (Korah) — Num. 16:35
32. Fire (Nadab, Abihu) — Lev. 10:2
33. The quail & plague — Num. 11:31-35
34. The murmuring & plague — Num. 16:41-50
35. Baal of Peor & plague — Num. 25:1-9
36. Aaron's rod blossoms — Num. 17:1-11
37. Brazen Serpent — Num. 21:6-9
38. Balaam's ass — Num. 22:22-33
39. God writes the commandments — Deut. 10:1-4
40. Moses mysterious burial — Deut. 34:1-8
41. Jordan divided — Josh. 3:14-17
42. Manna ceased — Josh. 5:12
43. Walls of Jericho fall — Josh. 6:1-20
44. Hailstones — Josh. 10:10,11
45. Sun standing still — Josh. 10:12-14

III. MIRACLES IN THE TIME OF THE JUDGES

46. Dew on Gideon's fleece — Judges 6:36-40
47. Water in jawbone for Samson — Judges 15:19

IV. MIRACLES IN THE TIME OF SAMUEL

48. Dagon falls — I Sam. 5:3-5
49. God answers by thunder — I Sam. 7:10

V. MIRACLES IN THE TIME OF THE PROPHET OF JUDAH

50. Jeroboam's hand withered — I Kings 13:4
51. The altar rent — I Kings 13:1-5

VI. MIRACLES IN THE TIME OF ELIJAH AND ELISHA

52. Fed by ravens — I Kings 17:4-6
53. Barrel of meal and cruse of oil — I Kings 17:12-16
54. Widow of Zarephath's son raised — I Kings 17:17-24
55. Answering by fire on Carmel — I Kings 18:20-39
56. Forty days sustained on Horeb — I Kings 19:8
57. Fire from heaven — II Kings 1:10-15
58. Elijah divides Jordan — II Kings 2:8
59. Elijah caught up — II Kings 2:11,12
60. Elisha divides Jordan — II Kings 2:13-15
61. Water healed — II Kings 2:19-22
62. Water given and victory over Moab — II Kings 3:16-20,22,23
63. Pot of Oil — II Kings 4:1-7
64. Shunammite's son raised — II Kings 4:20-37
65. Pottage healed — II Kings 4:38-41
66. Food multiplied — II Kings 4:42-44
67. Naaman healed — II Kings 5:1-14
68. Gehazi smitten — II Kings 5:27
69. Axe-head restored — II Kings 6:5-7
70. King's words repeated — II Kings 6:8-12
71. Horses and chariots shown — II Kings 6:15-17
72. Syrians smitten with blindness and restored — II Kings 6:18-20
73. Syrians flee at the sound of chariots — II Kings 7:6,7
74. Dead man raised — II Kings 13:20,21

VII. MIRACLES IN THE TIME OF ISAIAH

75. Sennacherib's host destroyed — II Kings 19:35; II Chron. 32:21; Isa. 37:36
76. The shadow returns — II Kings 20:9-11; II Chron. 32:24; Isa. 38:8

VIII. MIRACLES IN THE TIME OF DANIEL

77. The fiery furnace — Dan. 3:18-27
78. Handwriting on the wall — Dan. 5:5
79. The lion's den — Dan. 6:16-23

The New Testament and Healing

The New Testament abounds with the message of healing. I have listed below the healings of our Lord as well as other references.

INDIVIDUAL HEALINGS BY JESUS

	Matthew	Mark	Luke	John
1. Nobleman's Son				4:46-54
2. Unclean spirit		1:21-29	4:31-37	
3. Simon's Mother-in-law	8:14-15	1:29-31	4:38-39	
4. A Leper	8:1-4	1:40-45	5:12-16	
5. Paralytic carried by four	9:1-9	2:1-12	5:17-26	
6. Sick man at the pool				5:2-18
7. Withered Hand	12:9-14	3:1-6	6:6-11	
8. Centurian's Servant	8:5-13		7:2-10	
9. Widow's Son raised			7:11-17	
10. Demoniacs at Gadara	8:28-34	5:1-20	8:26-36	
11. Issue of blood	9:20-22	5:25-34	8:43-48	
12. Jairus' daughter raised	9:18,19; 23-25	5:22-24; 35-43	8:41,42; 49-56	
13. Two blind men	9:27-31			
14. Dumb devil possessed	9:32-34			
15. Daughter of Canaan woman	15:21-28	7:25-30		
16. Deaf. speech impediment		7:32-37		
17. Blind man of Bethesaida		8:22-26		
18. Epileptic boy	17:14-21	9:14-29	9:37-42	
19. Man born blind				9:1-38
20. Man blind, dumb, possessed	12:22-30		11:14-26	
21. Woman bent double			13:10-17	
22. Man with dropsy			14:1-5	
23. Raising of Lazarus				11:1-44
24. Ten Lepers			17:11-19	
25. Blind Bartimaeus	20:29-34	10:45-52	18:35-43	

MULTIPLE HEALINGS BY JESUS

	Matthew	Mark	Luke
1. Crowd at Peter's door	8:16-17	1:32-34	4:40-41
2. Crowds after leper healed			5:15
3. Crowd near Capernaum	12:15-21	3:7-12	5:17-26
4. Answering John's question	11:2-6		7:18-23
5. Before feeding the 5,000	14:13-14		9:11
6. At Gennesaret	14:34-36	6:53-55	
7. Before feeding 4,000	15:29-31		
8. Crowds beyond the Jordan	19:1-2		
9. Blind & lame in temple	21:14		
10. Some sick of Nazareth	13:53-58	6:1-6	
11. All kinds of sickness	4:23	6:56	
12. Every sickness & disease	9:35		
13. All oppressed (Acts 10:38)			

INDIVIDUAL HEALINGS BY THE APOSTLES

	Acts
1. The Lame man from birth	3:1-12
2. Paul regains his sight	9:10-22; 22:11-13
3. Aeneas the paralytic	9:32-35
4. Raising of Dorcas	9:36-42
5. Crippled man by Lystra	14:8-18
6. Girl with a spirit of divination	16:16-18
7. Eutychus restored to life	20:7-12
8. Paul healed of snake-bite	28:1-6
9. Father of Publius healed	28:7-8

MULTIPLE HEALINGS BY THE APOSTLES

1. Many wonders and signs	2:43
2. Many sick healed in Jerusalem	5:12-16
3. Stephen performs many miracles	6:8
4. Philip heals many at Samaria	8:5-13
5. Paul & Barnabas work signs and wonders	14:3
6. Paul heals at Ephesus	19:11-12
7. Sick healed at Melita	28:9

SOME OTHER NEW TESTAMENT SCRIPTURES

1. Instructions of Jesus & promises to Believers	Mk. 6:7; Mt. 10:5-8 Mark 16:14-20; Luke 10:8-9
2. Signs and wonders	Rom. 15:18-19; II Cor. 12:12; Heb. 2:4
3. Healing	I Cor. 12:9; 12:28-30 Rev. 22:2; I Peter 2:24
4. Anointing	Mark 6:13; James 5:14
5. Perfect eternal healing	Rev. 21:4

SOME OLD TESTAMENT REFERENCES TO HEALING

1. None of these diseases	Exodus 15:26
2. The fiery serpent	Numbers 21:6-9
3. Schunammite's son raised	II Kings 4:18-37
4. Naaman healed	II Kings 5:1-14
5. Hezekiah healed	II Kings 20:1-11
6. "With His stripes we are healed"	Isaiah 53:5
7. Some Healing Psalms	Psalm 23, 30, 103
8. Dead man raised	II Kings 13:20-21

Laying-On-Of-Hands

There are many Scripture references concerning the *"touch of the Master's hand."* For instance, *"And Jesus put forth His hand, and touched him."* Mt. 8:3. Also consider Matthew 8:1-4, 14-15, 9:13-15; Mark I 28-31, 40-45, 5:21-43, 6:1-6, 7:32-37, 8:22-24, 9:14-29, 10:13-16, 10:16-18; Luke 4:38-44, 5:12-15, 8:49-56, 13:11-17.

THE CHURCH'S HERITAGE

It is obvious that the Laying-on-of-Hands has been a part of the Christian Church from its beginning. Jesus Christ by precept and example set the pattern. His disciples and the members of the early Church followed His leading.

The passing centuries saw a transition to the point that the Laying-on-of-Hands was associated only with ordination of pastors, elders, deacons, and confirmation of new members.

Recent years have witnessed a new emphasis of Laying-on-of-Hands as a channel of the Lord's power for healing. This unique ministry of the Church has for far too long been neglected. It is refreshing to see the revival of this vital, scriptural, and timely ministry.

AN EXPRESSION OF BELIEF

Laying-on-of-Hands is a tangible expression of one's belief in the Great Physician. The one administering and the one receiving this ministry of the Church are both acknowledging dependence upon the Truine God for all healing.

God uses many concerned hands for our well-being. He uses the human touch whether it be the hands of skilled surgeons, a dedicated nurse, a sympathetic physician, the pastor, or a concerned lay person. His healing is extended through each.

The sad tragedy is that far too often the Church has abandoned the power of spiritual forces and left all ministry unto the ill to science. Science may complement spiritual ministries, but can never replace them.

THE FOCAL POINT

The focal point of Laying-on-of-Hands with prayer is the Lord Jesus Christ. The power does not come from the one laying on hands. The power is from the One in whose Name the prayer is offered. The believer serves only as a channel of Christ's power.

WHO IS WORTHY?

Worthiness does not lie in the individual but in the Lord Jesus. No one will ever arrive at the point of spiritual commitment which will make him or her worthy. One's willingness to administer through the Laying-on-of-Hands comes out of our obedience and not our purity.

There are some who feel only the professional clergy should lay on hands. I was in a large church conducting a healing service and the Pastor told me they did not encourage lay persons in this ministry.

This to me is teaching which will stifle the healing ministry. Lay persons can and should be instructed in this vital ministry and provided opportunity to fulfill this ministry.

I seek to teach lay persons to minister with the laying on of hands. They should not be denied this opportunity of service unto the Lord and to others.

HOW OFTEN?

How often should one receive Laying-on-of-Hands with prayer? At least weekly is the best answer I know. During periods of serious illness or problems some will desire this ministry daily

We haven't done all we can for ourselves and others until we have received this ministry of the Church. Since everyone constantly faces problems and also has deep concern for many friends and acquaintances, taking advantage of an opportunity to pray and to receive Laying-on-of-Hands with prayer regarding these situations is an act of wisdom as well as obedience.

Your prayer and devotional life will be enhanced and your faith and trust increased as you minister unto others and others minister unto you through the Laying-on-of-Hands with prayer.

You and yours will be blessed as you receive the *"touch of the Master's hands"* through others.

Laying-On-Of-Hands (con't)

THE OLD TESTAMENT

There are two reasons for LOH as mentioned in the Old Testament.

1. The blessing of an heir (Gen. 48:14)
2. Empowering of a leader, Joshua in (Deut. 34:9) and Joash (II Kings 13:16)

THE NEW TESTAMENT

The LOH are included among the foundations of faith along with repentance, faith, baptisms, resurrection, and judgment. (Heb. 6:1-3)

The New Testament mentions the LOH for the following occasions:

1. Ordination of deacons (Acts 6:6)
2. To receive the Holy Spirit (Acts 8:17; 19:6)
3. For the commissioning of missionaries Acts 13:3)
4. To impart spiritual gifts (I Tim. 4:14; II Tim. 1:6)
5. For healing (Mk. 16:17,18; James 5:14-15)

THE CHURCH

Through the centuries the Institutional Church has faithfully practiced LOH for ordination, commissioning missionaries and confirmation but sadly neglected LOH for the sick and troubled. Since New Testament practices produce New Testament results, LOH for the ill and troubled should be a part of the ministry of every congregation.

There is no magic to LOH. There are truths to be considered and I present the following guidelines. They may be called the ABC's of LOH.

A. ACCEPT GOD'S DESIRE

God wants the very best for you. He does not delight in your illnesses, afflictions, and problems. On the contrary, His message is to obey His laws and be spared these things. The Kingdom of Heaven is at hand and you are invited to enter and to abide there. Most people believe God is able to create a vast universe. However, they have difficulty believing He can care for their little problems. I encourage you to accept the fact that the Lord of Creation is the Lord of every detail of your life.

B. BELIEVE THE LORD IS YOUR SOURCE

The Lord may use many and varied instruments to meet your every need. However, He is the Source of all. Your apparently unsolvable problems or incurable disease is solvable or curable in God's sight. He has power and resources available you never dreamed existed and will never experience until you believe He will supply your every need. (Phil. 4:19) The one ministering LOH unto you is not your source of help and healing, but only the channel of God's power and purpose.

C. CONFESS YOUR NEED

Confession is a two-sided coin. First, it speaks of your inability to heal yourself. This you must acknowledge and accept. It may be obvious that physically you fall short of perfection and wholeness, but true confession acknowledges falling short of the Glory of God in all areas. Honesty is one of the biggest steps toward healing of body, mind, and spirit.

Pride keeps many from God's wholeness. Confession is not only good for the soul, but also for the body. The publican's prayer could very well be paraphrased, *"God be merciful to me the sick one."* (Luke 18:13)

D. CONFESS YOUR FAITH

The other side of the coin of confession is your witness to others. LOH is a confession to others of your faith in the Triune God.

The Lord has promised to honor, now and in the world to come, your public confession of Him. (Mt. 10:32)

LOH is not given or received for show, but is a public expression of inward faith. It is one way, among many, whereby you can say to the Church and the world that you are not ashamed of the Master nor His methods. His desire is your wholeness. Believe Him today!

Healing — God's Gift

Each year we celebrate the Birthday of our Lord. We do not claim that He was born December 25th. No one can be certain as to the exact day or date.

One thing we do know is that He was and is the Son of God. We need to be reminded again and again that He was born into this world for each of us.

GOD'S GIFT

The Babe in Bethlehem's manger was God's gift to the world. Thus He is God's gift to you and to people everywhere and for all time.

God is desirous that His gift be received in each heart. It is through His gift that you receive the gifts of redemption, forgiveness, and healing. None of these are earned. They are freely given by the Father of all love.

> *"Every good gift and every perfect gift is from above, and cometh down from the Father of lights, with whom is no variableness, neither shadow of turning."* (James 1:17)

> *"If ye then, being evil, know how to give good gifts unto your children how much more shall your father in heaven give good things to them that ask him?"* (Matthew 7:11)

> *"I am come that they might have life, and that they might have it more abundant."* (John 10:10)

The abundant life includes health of body and mind and spirit.

Wholeness, healing, and health have the same basic root meaning in Greek. The Apostolic Church knew and believed that one of God's gifts was healing.

> *"...to another the gifts of healing by the same Spirit."* (I Cor. 12:9)

The first Christians believed and lived-out the divine commission to preach, teach, and heal. They believed in the Power of God and thus possessed the Power of God.

RECEIVING THE GIFT

If healing is a gift of the Lord, the natural question is, *"How do I receive this gift?"*

A big step toward the receiving of the gift of healing is to understand the spiritual laws. They have been given to us to help us appropriate the blessings of the Lord.

> *"But his delight is in the law of the Lord; and in his law doth he meditate day and night."* (Psalm 1:2)

The spiritual laws are not temporarily suspended just for you. The natural laws are not changed with our whims and fancies. It would be foolish to jump from a tall building believing that gravity would be altered. The Lord tells us there are spiritual laws which are essential to our wholeness and receiving all He has for us. I mention two of them.

1. BELIEF

Belief is a spiritual law of utmost importance. Jesus said,

> *"All things are possible to him who believes."* (Mark 9:23)

> *"What things soever ye desire, when ye pray, believe that ye receive them, and ye shall have them."* (Mark 11:24)

2. FORGIVENESS

Another spiritual law is forgiveness. This is the only point which Jesus expounded upon after He had given His disciples His model prayer. (Mt. 6:14,15)

CONCLUSION

God's Gift, His Son, is not received to be selfishly used or misused. You receive the Gift that you may impart the Gift.

Share God's Gift for your health's sake.

Paul's Thorn in the Flesh

"...There was given to me a thorn in the flesh" (II Cor. 12:7) has been a controversial statement through the centuries.

A PHYSICAL MALADY?

The commonly accepted interpretation of this verse is that Paul had a physical malady and that the Lord gave the problem and then refused to remove it.

I feel this verse can be either a stumbling block or a stepping stone as far as the message of healing is concerned. It all depends upon your interpretation of the total message of the Bible.

SEARCH THE SCRIPTURES

A careful consideration of Scripture provides provocative material for another insight concerning Paul's *"thorn in the flesh."*

Does *"thorn in the flesh"* necessarily mean a physical illness? The answer is a resounding NO!

The Old Testament has three references using similar language as Paul does in II Cor. 12:7.

1. Num. 33:55 speaks of *"...thorns in your sides"*
2. Jos. 23:13 says, *"scourges in your sides and thorns in your eyes"*
3. Judg. 2:3 refers to *"...thorns in your sides"*

It is evident from the context that these three references do not imply physical illnes. They very definitely refer to the pagan and carnal inhabitants of the land Israel is to conquer.

Paul had great knowledge of the Old Testament and was steeped in Jewish ways of expression. It would be natural for him to use this familiar phrase to refer to those who troubled him and hindered the advance of the Good News.

THE FLESH

The word translated *"flesh"* in II Cor. 12:7 is the same as the word for *"flesh"* used by Paul in many other places. He meant by *"flesh"* any and all things which were contrary to the nature and will of God. See Rom. 7:5, 18; 8:1-3. Thus, *"flesh"* does not necessariy mean one's body.

PROBLEM PEOPLE

Paul, like the early Hebrew children, was plagued with problem people. They very well could have been his *"thorn in the flesh."*

It was because of them that he often had great difficulty preaching the Gospel. He was never completely delivered from those who followed him wherever he went and constantly fermented strife. They may have served to keep him humble, but they were also a hindrance to the advancement of the Church.

Paul's human weaknesses were more pointedly manifest in the face of the opposition from such people. This concept certainly brings an understanding to II Cor. 12:10. *"Therefore I take pleasure in infirmities, in reproaches, in necessities, in persecutions, in distresses for Christ's sake, for when I am weak, then I am strong."*

SATAN — THE MESSENGER

Anyone who wants to defend his illness by hiding behind the *"thorn in the flesh"* theory faces another problem. Some leave the impression that the Lord has made them ill to keep them humble and dependent upon Him.

This is a subtle way for a person to infer that they may be a special case before the Lord. Thus the illness is almost turned into proof of being a favorite in the Lord's sight. What a strange twist to the total message of Scripture.

The verse, II Cor. 12:7, plainly identifies the messenger of the *"thorn in the flesh"* as Satan. This is a far cry from its being from God. If one interprets that the *"thorn in the flesh"* is a physical illness, then he must acknowledge it is from Satan. God's gift and God's will is not illness.

WHOLENESS — GOD'S WILL

I pray you will believe and acknowledge that illness is not from God. God wants to defeat illness, not deliver it. Jesus faithfully fulfilled the Father's will and He *"...healed them all."* Luke 6:19.

Medicine and Spiritual Healing

"Man operates — God heals," is a well known statement in medical circles. Indeed, God is the Healer. Man, in whatever capacity, is only a channel of his healing.

FALSE CONCEPTS

There are many false concepts concerning healing. I want to mention two prevalent ones.

1. *"If I had enough faith I would never be ill or need to see a physician."*

2. *"Prayer is only psychological and has no place as far as physical disease is concerned."*

Both of the above are extreme and false statements.

MEDICAL HELP

The proper services of the physician and the proper use of medicine are as Christian as prayer meetings and Bible Study. Often sincere and devout Christians have a sense of guilt if they seek the ministry of a physician. *"If only I had more faith, I would be immediately healed,"* is almost constantly on the mind of such individuals.

I feel this is wrong. All need to hear and to understand that the Spiritual Healing Ministry recognizes and appreciates God's healing through physicians and medicines. Medical insights and belief in the Healing Christ are not contradictory. In fact, many of the most ardent devotees of the validity of the Spiritual Healing Ministry are physicians, nurses, and others in the allied professions of healing.

In like manner, the leaders in the area of the Spiritual Healing Ministry do not hesitate to seek the services of physicians. They realize that when a person seeks the services of a physician this does not deny the presence and power of the healing Christ.

WHAT IS THE ANSWER

In a nutshell the message of Spiritual Healing is that an individual has not done all that can be done until —

1. You have prayed.
2. You have prayed with other believers.
3. You have been prayed for by others.
4. You have sought the best professional help available.

ABUSE THE PROBLEM

Abuse, not use, is the problem regarding the many channels of healing. Spiritual Healing is not a matter of pills vs. prayer. It is the improper use of any of the above which is wrong.

Some by their own volition or through the encouragement of others have thrown away their pills and/or stopped seeing their physician. Many have suffered immeasurably from such foolishness.

However, the other side of the coin is that millions are looking only to the physicians and pills as the answer to their illnesses. They neglect the spiritual.

GUIDELINES

A few sensible guidelines concerning medicine and Spiritual Healing are worthy of your consideration.

1. Appreciate that the Lord is the Healer regardless of the channel used.

2. Realize that the field of medicine will never have the complete answer to problems or to illness.

3. Acknowledge that humanness involves spirit as well as physical aspects.

4. Don't lean on the wonders of medicine as a crutch for your problems. There are no *"magic"* pills for any and all illnesses.

5. Realize that the healing of the spirit is the most important goal. Even Jesus told His enthused followers, *"...rejoice not, that the spirits are subject unto you, but rather rejoice, because your names are written in heaven."* (Lu. 10:20) There are many mysterious and unexplainable physical healings. However, the greatest and most mysterious of all healings are of the spirit.

6. Give thanks and praise unto the Lord for His healings regardless of the method or channel He may use.

7. Pray for all who are in any way involved in the ministry of healing. This should include pastors, lay persons, physicians, nurses, psychiatrists, researchers, administrators, laundry help, etc.

8. Faithfully participate in Spiritual Healing services and believe the Lord is willing and able to meet your every need. He is most willing that you come unto Him. You acknowledge publicly your willingness to come through participation in the services.

The Weakness of Medicine

It was my privilege to hear Dr. C. B. King, M.D. present the message, *"The Weakness of Medicine,"* at the meeting of the International Order of St. Luke the Physician.

MY MEDICAL BACKGROUND

Dr. King began by saying, I love medicine. I have no intention of disparaging medicine. I am quite cognizant of the great medical progress over the last fifty years and I am proud to be a member of the medical profession.

I practiced medicine for 36 years without knowing that the Church had a healing ministry. That the Church is involved in healing was certainly never mentioned in medical school nor was it ever mentioned from the pulpit, and I was a regular church attender.

The healing miracles were confined to New Testament times. I took no stock in the healings claimed by the Christian Scientist or the so called Faith Healers. For me the practice of medicine and the ministry of the Church had nothing in common; they were separated as far as the East is from the West.

For me medicine was complete, independent, and self-sufficient. The Church had nothing to offer except prayers for the forgiveness of sins and the last rites.

APOSTOLIC CHURCH

The ministry of the early Apostolic Church was to the whole man. In those days the priest and the physician were often the same man. There was faith but not science in medicine until the time of Hippocrates. For some 300 years the Church ministered to the whole man.

A GREAT GULF

At this time, due to lack of faith and other causes the healing ministry of the Church gradually died out. The Church became involved with the spirit only and science became involved with the body and the mind.

Thus a wide gulf was formed between medicine and the Church and a weakness developed in the ministry of both the Church and medicine in that neither considered man as a whole person — body, soul and spirit. In spite of the great scientific advancements that medicine has made in the past fifty years, this weakness persists.

I wish to point out this weakness in medicine.

THE WEAKNESS

1. Medicine is weak when it fails to consider disease of the spirit as an underlying cause of disease of soul and body.

2. Medicine is weak when it fails to include the Healing Ministry of the Church alongside scientific skills in the treatment of disease.

3. Medicine is weak when it fails to recognize man as a spiritual being.

4. Medicine is weak when it fails to communicate through prayer with the source of all power and healing — Jesus Christ.

5. Medicine is weak because it is on a horizontal plane. It is humanistic and materialistic.

6. Medicine is weak when it fails to recognize the presence of the Lord Jesus Christ to praise Him and to thank Him.

MAN A TRINITY

Since man is a trinity there must be close cooperation between medicine and the Church if the whole man is to be healed.

LET'S COOPERATE

I was called to see a patient at her home. She was in very poor health, having just recently returned from the hospital.

I felt that this patient needed something more than the ointment for her eye. I suggested that she call the pastor of a church nearby — one whom I knew to be a believer in the Healing Ministry of the Church — and ask him to come and anoint her with oil and pray for her healing.

Then she told me that she was a member of this church and that she would be happy to follow my suggestions.

The pastor complied with her request and came weekly to anoint her with oil and pray for her healing.

And this is the way it should be, my friends, the physician and the pastor, each ministering to the patient in his own way, cooperating for the best interests of the whole person.

Note: Dr. King's complete message concerning "The Weakness of Medicine" may be purchased in booklet form from Life Enrichment Publishers, Box 526, Canton, Ohio 44701.

Spiritual Healing Throughout the Centuries

The New Testament abounds with references to healings.

Did the power of healing cease with the death of the apostles? Were the first generation of Christians the only ones who were to witness the healing power of our Lord? Are we to believe that the healings of the Great Physician were for the Apostolic Age only?

THROUGH THE CENTURIES

Believers may respond with a NO to all of the above questions. The church through the ages has had a healing witness. It at times has waned, but it has never disappeared.

Perhaps most Christians of any age are reluctant to fully appropriate the power of the Lord. However, there are always the bold and believing souls who stand out as great examples of the power of the Lord to heal.

JUSTIN MARTYR (165 A. D.)

"For numberless demoniacs throughout the whole world and in your city, many of our Christian men, exorcising them in the Name of Jesus Christ, who was crucified under Pontius Pilate have healed, and do heal, rendering helpless and driving the possessing devils out of the men though they could not be cured by all the other exorcists and those who used incantations and drugs."

IRENAEUS (200 A. D.)

"Those who are in truth His disciples, receiving grace from Him, do in His name perform miracles; and they truly cast out devils. Others still heal the sick by laying on their hands upon them, and they are made whole. Yes, moreover, as I have said, the dead even have been raised up, and remained among us for many years."

ORIGEN (250 A. D.)

"And some give evidence of their having received through their faith a marvelous power by the cures which they perform, invoking no other name over those who need their help than that of the God of all things, and of Jesus, along with a mention of His history. For by these means we too have seen many persons freed from grievous calamities, and from distractions of mind, and madness, and countless other ills, which could be cured neither by men or devils."

CLEMENT (275 A. D.)

"Let them (young ministers), therefore with fasting and prayer, make their intercessions, and not with the well arranged, and fitly ordered words of learning, but as men who have received the gift of healing confidently, to the glory of God."

THEODORE OF MOPUCSTE (429 A. D.)

"Many heathen amongst us are being healed by Christians from whatever sickness they have, so abundant are miracles in our midst."

MARTIN LUTHER (1483-1546)

"The tax collector in Torgau and the councilor in Belgern have written me to ask that I offer some good advice for Mr. John Korner, afflicted husband. I know of no worldly help to give. If the physicians are at a loss to find a remedy, you may be sure that it is not a case of ordinary melancholy. It must rather, be an affliction that comes from the devil, and this must be counteracted by the power of Christ and with the prayer of faith. This is what we do, and that we have been accustomed to do, for a cabinet maker here was similarly afflicted with madness and we cured him by prayer in Christ's Name."

ZINSENDORF (1700-1760)

"To believe against hope is the root of the gift of miracles and I owe this testimony to our beloved church, that Apostolic powers are there manifested. We have undeniable proofs thereof which could not humanly have been discovered, in the healing of maladies in themselves incurable, such as cancers, consumptions, when the patient was in the agencies of death, all by means of prayer, or of a single word."

TODAY

We live in an age which is again seeing the power of the Lord through the ministry of healing. The Great Physician invites each believer to accept His invitation to wholeness. He also wants us to impart it to others.

Heralds of Healing

Christ has revealed His desire for your wholeness. It is the wholeness of body, mind, and spirit which He wants to impart to you and to others.

It is tragic that many have not heard this glad and good message. The following two comments illustrate that countless thousands have not heard the good news that Jesus Christ is the Great Physician.

> *"If I had known of Spiritual Healing years ago, I could have survived some very frustrating working conditions of the past."*

> *"It seems to me that this area (healing) has been sadly neglected by many churches. I was reared in a church and never heard the subject discussed as being relevant to our day."*

AN EFFECTIVE HERALD

Each believer should strive to become an effective herald of the message of healing. You have the opportunity to learn and to share concerning God's desire for wholeness. The following suggestions will serve to guide you in your pilgrimage to being a herald of His healing presence and power.

BOOKS

There are many good books concerning healing. I would urge you to read them. Your knowledge of healing will be increased and you can share your knowledge and books with others.

This book, **The Adventures of Healing**, is an excellent book to share with others. It presents insights for the novice as well as the one advanced in their knowledge of healing.

INVITATION

There is no more effective teaching than experience. Therefore, I suggest you invite your friends to attend a healing service with you.

A CONFERENCE

You can be a herald of healing by inviting individuals to attend a healing conference. It would be great if you paid the expenses of your pastor to a healing conference.

COURSE ON HEALING

Many congregations have discovered that a course on healing has helped provide a firm foundation for a healing ministry. The course may be presented during Sunday School or at any convenient hour. **The Adventures of Healing** is excellent for a course book.

GUEST SPEAKERS

You and your church will be blessed by guest speakers in the area of healing. They can share their experiences. Some can effectively present strengths and blessings, pitfalls and problems, mechanics and methods of a healing ministry.

PUBLICITY

You and your congregation can be more effective heralds of healing through good publicity.

The church bulletin, parish paper, pulpit announcements, newspaper releases, tracts, pamphlets, books, etc. all are avenues for letting others know that the Lord heals today.

SPIRITUAL HEALING SUNDAY

A Spiritual Healing Sunday can be a time of learning for a large percentage of the active members of your congregation.

Sunday School teachers and others will have to study concerning healing to present it to their students on this day. Thus it serves as a marvelous tool to deeper understanding of healing.

THE SCRIPTURES

I encourage you to study the scriptures in the light of the healing message. You will be surprised how the Bible comes alive when you begin to really believe that the Great Physician heals today.

PRAYER

I hope you will pray for the Lord to guide you in the area of healing. Pray for yourself, for others who minister healing, for those unto whom you and others will minister. You and all believers are to be faithful heralds of healing.

Anointing with Oil

Anointing is mentioned many times in the Bible.

	Old Testament	New Testament
Anoint	30 times	5 times
Anoited	86 times	12 times
Anointest	2 times	0
Anointing	25 times	3 times

WHY ANOINT?

It is obvious that anointing with oil was very much a part of Biblical practices. The following are some of the reasons for anointing.

1. Consecration of leaders - Ex. 28:41; I Sam. 16:12.
2. God's chosen ones - Ps. 2:2, 18:50.
3. Empowerment - Isa. 61:1.
4. Spirit of gladness - Heb. 1:9
5. The sick - Mk. 6:13; Jam. 5:14

POST-APOSTOLIC CHURCH

It is a shame that the post-Apostolic Church declined spiritually. This decline resulted in many of the practices of the early Christian community being neglected, ignored, or distorted.

For instance, the anointing with oil became associated with death rather than with healing. Anointing became a last rite before death instead of a sacred act of faith leading to restoration to health.

The Council of Florence in 1435 gave the kiss of death to the true significance of anointing with oil. It ruled that oil could only be used for the sacrament of Extreme Unction. Through the centuries most Catholics and many Protestants have accepted this position.

NEW INTEREST

I am thrilled at the intense interest in healing which is in all branches of the Christian church today. Basically this is happening because of the outpouring of the Holy Spirit and the new awareness of His presence and power. There is a new eagerness to know the scripture and to renew the practices of the early Church.

DON'T GET SIDETRACKED

Biblically, anointing with oil has strong support. Practically, anointing with oil tangibly speaks to the ill and troubled of the love of Christ and His desire to heal.

It also brings more meaning and significance to intercessory prayer.

It is sad to note that some become sidetracked in this ministry because they become entangled in details and controversy. They become more disturbed as to whom should do it, how, when, where, etc. These real or imagined barriers deter them from administering this sacred rite.

I feel the heart of the matter is that every effort should be expended to inform individuals of the value and efficacy of anointing with oil. Lay persons and clergy should be involved in this important and biblical ministry.

ASK TO BE ANOINTED

Every believer bears the responsibility of requesting to be anointed when ill. You have not done all you can for yourself or an ill loved one if you neglect being anointed with oil.

Few pastors or officers of a congregation will refuse to honor a sincere request for anointing. As a believer you have the privilege and responsibility to call upon the leadership of your congregation for anointing.

TEACH ANOINTING

Pastors and other church leaders must teach concerning anointing with oil. Some pastors and lay persons may say, *"If someone were to ask me to anoint with oil I would. I never suggest or encourage it."* This is a cute cop-out.

How can anyone ask for what they do not know exists? How can members of a congregation know of anointing with oil unless someone teaches them?

The disciples of our Lord had no hesitancy to use oil. (Mk. 6:13) He instructed them to do so.

If a person refuses to request anointing after being informed that one bears the burden of neglect. If a person is never enlightened then his instructor bears the burden of guilt.

Spiritual Healing and Holy Communion

There are many Christians who believe that the Holy Communion is a beautiful service to be occasionally observed. It is to them more pageantry than power.

We need to be reminded again and again of the proper understanding of Holy Communion.

The Bible says, *"My people are destroyed for lack of knowledge..."* (Ho. 4:6) There is no area where knowledge seems to be lacking more than with Holy Communion.

St. Paul points out the seriousness of improperly receiving the elements. He says it results in illness and sometimes even death. (I Cor. 11:29,30)

KORBANA

The New Testament was originally written in Aramaic, which was the language Jesus and His followers used.

Communion is a word derived from the Aramaic word *Korbana*. It means offering or sacrifice and it comes from an Aramaic root which means draw near.

You never draw nearer to the source of all power than you do when you partake of the Holy Communion. How important to you and yours that you draw near in a worthy manner.

NOT AN OPTION

Holy Communion is an open invitation to power and wholeness. It is not an option for a believer.

It is a visible expression of the deep inward assurance of the love and power of the Lord Jesus Christ. (Mt. 26:26-29; Mk. 14:17-25; Lu. 22:14-23; I Cor. 11:17-30)

NOT MAGIC

The ordinances and practices of the Christian faith are never matters to be simply mechanically observed. They were instituted to help us appropriate the power of the Lord.

There is no magic in the Holy Communion or any other aspect of Christian worship. We are called unto the Lord and not to ritual.

CHRIST YOUR STRENGTH

Christ's body was a healthy body. It was a spirit filled body. He was a vessel unto complete honor to His Father.

Christ is your healer. The prophet tells us that in His body He bore even our diseases. *"But he was wounded for our transgressions, he was bruised for our iniquities: the chastisement of our peace was upon him; and with his stripes we are healed."* (Isa. 53:5)

WHEN YOU COMMUNE

The next time you partake of Holy Communion please keep the following in mind.

1. The purpose of Christ - Christ came that you might have wholeness in all areas of life. (Jn. 10:10) This wholeness includes the forgiveness of your sin. (Mk. 10:45) He also desires your wholeness of body and mind. (Mk. 1:21-28)

2. The power of Christ - Christ made this vast universe from nothing. (Heb. 11:1-3) All the forces of nature and even Satan are subject unto Him. (Mt. 8:27; Mk. 4:41, 1:27) He is coming again in power to reign forever and ever. (Acts 1:11)

3. The presence of Christ - Christ is more than someone who lived, expressed His feelings, propounded His theology and theories and then died. He is alive forever more. He lives within each believer. He will be with His church to the end of this age and beyond. (Mt. 28:20)

The presence of Christ is more than a nebulous thought. It is a real experience and assurance of His love. You are in Christ and He is in you.

The Holy Communion is a continuing life line to Life Himself. Appropriate His healing power as you receive the Bread and the Cup.

Prayer and Spiritual Healing

The Bible certainly conveys the importance of prayer. For instance —

"...Men ought always to pray and not to faint." (Lu. 18:1)

"Pray without ceasing." (I Th. 5:17)

"...the effectual fervent prayer of a righteous man availeth much." (Jam. 5:16)

DEEP COMMUNION

Prayer is the deep communion and precious fellowship of the believer with the Triune God. This relationship is esential. *"It is Thee and not Thy gifts I crave."* Matheson.

NOT MAGIC

Prayer is more than seeking to move God to fulfill our selfish desires. It is not magic. It is not a tool to be used only in a *"pinch."*

It is not simply an avenue for seeking special favors from the Lord, nor the key to changing God's mind.

CONVERSATION

Brother Lawrence presents a beautiful insight concerning prayer when he speaks of it as a continual conversation with God.

"There is not in the world a kind of life more sweet and delightful than that of a continual conversation with God. Those only can comprehend it who practice and experience it."

BREATH OF THE SPIRIT

Prayer is more than passive contemplation. It is the spirit of the Living God being very much a part of you. It is you relating to the Lord in the most meaningful way possible.

William James has well said that prayer *"is the very soul and essence of religion"* and without prayer there *"is no intimate commerce, no interior dialogue, no interchange, no action of God in man, no return of man to God."*

PRAYER AND HEALING

Spiritual Healing without prayer is like a body without the breath of life. Every believer must realize that no one has done all he can about any problem or illness until he has prayed. Also, he should pray with others and be prayed for and ministered unto with prayer by others.

This emphasis upon prayer is in no way a suggestion that professional help should be ignored or neglected.

AID TO HEALING

Even in physical distress prayer is vital. Dr. Alexis Carrel has written, *"A doctor who sees a patient give himself to prayer can indeed rejoice. The calm engendered by prayer is a powerful aid to healing. It appears indispensable to our highest development."*

PRAYER SUGGESTIONS

Below are some practical ways to make prayer a vital part of the Spiritual Healing Ministry.

1. Each believer spending time each day in prayer and meditation.

2. Developing and maintaining prayer groups in cooperation with other churches.

3. Prayer chains for urgent requests.

4. Intercessory prayer time at the healing service.

5. A book in which prayer requests may be entered as they are received.

6. Each believer maintaining his own prayer list of specific needs. Many have discovered my book, *"Personal Prayer List,"* a very practical tool for this purpose.

IT WORKS

Prayer is a most practical and powerful force. It does work. Pray today!

Practical Prayers

Prayer is essential. It is essential not because it is to enable us to do the work of the church. It is essential because it is the work of the church.

PRACTICAL

Tennyson vividly presented the practicality and importance of prayer as follows:

> *"More things are wrought by prayer than this world dreams of. Wherefore, let thy voice rise like a fountain for me night and day. For what are men better than sheep or goats; That nourish a blind life within the brain, If knowing God, they lift not hands of prayer. Both for themselves and those who call them friend."*

The disciples of our Lord must have seen prayer as a very practical and powerful part of the life of our Lord. We have no record of them asking Him to teach them to organize, teach, preach, or even evangelize. However, they did ask, *"Lord, teach us how to pray."* (Lu. 11:1)

A VITAL PRAYER LIFE

You can develop a more vital prayer life. It is imperative that you do so. It is the one aspect of Christian devotion which can be done anytime, anywhere, and by anyone.

Prayer knows no barriers. It can circle our globe in an instant. It is possible through prayer to enter prisons, lift distant loved ones unto the Lord, and to enter into impossible situations. This power should not be neglected by you or by any believer.

PRACTICAL PRAYERS

Below are two very practical prayers which will help you minister unto yourself and to others.

1. Affirmation - The Lord has invited you unto Himself. You need to affirm in your own heart the faith the Lord has given to you. Therefore, I suggest this prayer.

"Precious Father, you are my creator and sustainer. You are Lord of my spirit, body, and mind. As your child I have been made alive in Christ Jesus. I am free from the law of sin and death.

"Holy Spirit, thank you for ever wanting to impart the assurance of your presence with me. Thank you for revealing to me the love, light, and peace of the Father. Thank you for continuing to cleanse, guide, and comfort me.

"Lord Jesus, I am grateful that I can open my life unto you as a channel of your healing life and love. Amen."

2. Intercession - I strongly encourage you to minister unto others through intercessory prayer. Prayers in intercession do not have to be long. I suggest the following:

"Father of all mercies, I pray for your wholeness for ...(name)... May he/she know your love in its fullness. Set him/her free from fears, distresses, and infirmities. I pray for ...(name)... in the Name of Christ our Great Physician. Amen."

After praying the above I would encourage you to reach out in prayer to the one for whom you are praying. The following prayer will help you do this.

"...(name)..., I am praying for you. I am praying that you will commit your life unto your loving heavenly Father. May you realize He is more willing to forgive, restore, refresh, and revive than you are to ask. I pray you will know that our Lord does not give you the spirit of fear, but of power, and of love and of a sound mind.

"...(name)..., be of good cheer. The Lord's love surrounds you. May His ways become your ways. May His precious peace pervade your being. May you lift your eyes from your problems to your Problem Solver, Jesus Christ. May His joy be within you, His radiance around you, His glory above you, and His everlasting arms underneath you.

"...(name)..., may these truths be grasped by you. May you never forsake them. These things I pray in the Name of Jesus Christ our Great Physician and through the power of the Holy Spirit. Amen."

The words of the prophet Samuel are fitting to consider when thinking of intercessory prayer. He said, *"God forbid that I should sin against the Lord in ceasing to pray for you."* (I Sam. 12:23)

According to Thy Will

"...I will; be thou clean," are the words of Jesus to the leper who approached Him saying, *"...if thou wilt, thou canst make me whole."* Christ's response was *"I will!"*

The Church today needs to emphasize that our Lord desires wholeness for His children.

ACCORDING TO THY WILL

It is going to take a great deal of teaching to counteract the centuries of false teaching of *"If it be Thy will."* This statement by our Lord dealt with total commitment to His high calling. It was never used by Him in relationship to an illness.

SUFFERING

Some will say, *"But so many are ill and there is so much suffering in the world. It must be God's will."* I do not want to gloss over the misery in this world. However, do we lay the blame for it at the feet of God?

I feel to blame God for this is a basic misunderstanding of the Creator and Sustainer of all life. Man's ignorance, failure to believe and to practice spiritual laws, and many other factors are involved in illness of body, soul and spirit.

It is God's will that we seek and expect His wholeness. This is as true as to believe that He wants all to come to repentance. All do not come, but we do not accuse God of not wanting them.

GOOD HEALTH — GOD'S WILL

Jesus never said to anyone, *"I'm going to make you ill so you will come to know the love of God in your life."* How ridiculous! On the contrary He healed the multitudes of their illnesses. Below are some good reasons why you can be certain God wants you well.

I. OUR FATHER

The very nature of our heavenly Father is that He is more concerned for our well-being than even ourselves or our parents and friends. *"If ye then, being evil know how to give good gifts unto your children, how much more shall your father which is in heaven give good things to them that ask Him?"* (Mt. 7:11)

II. JESUS CHRIST

The very nature of Jesus Christ necessitates His ministering to meet your needs. He not only wants you to forgive your sins, but He also wants to heal your diseases.

Jesus saw both illness and sin as of the Evil one and thus to be defeated. He not only said to the paralytic that his sins were forgiven, but he was also told to rise and walk. (Mk. 2:1-12)

The Christian Church has always taught that Christ perfectly obeyed the Father. He would not do anything contrary to His Father's will. Since much of His minstry was healing, how can anyone say that wholeness is not God's will?

III. THE BODY

Your very body is made for wholeness. Attacked by an alien the defenses of your body immediately go into action. They strive to ward off the disease and to restore wholeness.

An infection in your body is the alarm alerting your lymphocytes to pour out antibodies and to call upon other cells to help. There may be as many as a million antibodies in your body. They are available when needed and each is equipped to fight a particular disease. Amazing, isn't it?

IV. APOSTOLIC CHURCH

The ministry of the Apostolic Church was one of helping and healing. It was not a ministry of helplessness and hopelessness in the face of illness.

Physical, mental and spiritual healings were an integral part of the Apostolic Church. The *"If it be thy will,"* approach crept into the life of the church as her faith and power faded. It was not part of its initial thrust, but a part of its later deficiencies and decay.

V. SCRIPTURE

The scriptural promises and instructions of the Lord Jesus attest to His desire for your wholeness (Mt. 10:1; Mk. 16:18; Lu. 9:1, 10:9)

The Good News was a message accompanied with much power. This is evident from many events in the life of the followers of our Lord. (Rom. 15:18,19; II Cor. 12:12; Heb. 2:4; I Cor. 12:9,12:28-30; I Pet. 2:24; Rev. 22:2)

The early Church often used anointing and prayer to heal the sick. (Jam. 5:14)

God's will is your health. Good health is God's will. Believe Him today! Your wholeness is according to His will. Amen.

There Are No Failures

The following witness by a physically afflicted individual is dynamic. *"I am lame, and I recall at the age of 15 I prayed (in church) for a physical miracle to make me walk straight like other people. My prayer was not answered in this way. Instead God gave me a fierce desire to avoid letting my lameness keep me from leading a full, rich, active life; spent as far as possible in helping others. I have done this!"*

NOT ONLY PHYSICAL

This person has grasped the real meaning of Spiritual Healing. So often when healing is under discussion the question arises, *"What about failures?"*

The question itself is indicative of the individual focusing primarily on the physical. Further evidence that most people think only of the physical is seen when a group is asked, *"Have any of you ever seen a miracle.?"*

Most will answer "NO" and those who answer "YES" will give an account of a physical healing they have witnessed or experienced. This emphasis upon the physical is natural. The physical can be easily seen and discerned.

Even the biblical accounts are usually concerning physical healings. They were the ones which impressed those who beheld the healing power of our Lord.

MAN MORE THAN PHYSICAL

When there is no physical healing, some people are ready to cry, *"God has failed me."*

Pause for a moment and consider. What really is Spiritual Healing? A person is more than a physical being. Every individual is also a mental and spiritual being.

The following diagram will help you to see that the person coming for healing has a multitude of problems and needs. The box represents the WHOLE person. The numbers represent the many facets of the life of the person.

1 2 4 6 3 7 5 8 9 10

COMPLEX NEEDS

Each number in the block represents an area of disease or difficulty in the life of the one receiving prayer.

The individual receiving Laying-on-of-Hands with prayer may have what appears to be: 1. Terminal cancer. However, this one also comes with —

2. fear of death
3. financial worries
4. concern for family
5. guilt of past sins and present doubt
6. worries of what will happen to his wife and children if he dies
7. despair as he questions, *"Why me?"*
8. *fear of losing his job*
9. *almost unbearable pain*
10. *physical weakness*

There is more than a person with a physical disease called cancer. This person has a multitude of problems.

ALWAYS HELPED

When there is no evidence of physical healing some people are ready to cry, *"God has failed me."*

This is undo emphasis upon a single factor of life. An individual may not be cured of cancer, but yet receive help in one or more of the other areas of deep concern.

The person may be healed of the cancer. However, the point is that when one comes for healing he is always helped and cured in some area.

Sincere prayer on the part of yourself and with others is imperative. There are no failures for those who sincerely seek the Lord and His healing touch.

PROPER FOCUS

The approach of a complete ministry to an individual brings Spiritual Healing into proper focus.

There are physical healings beyond explanation. We call them miracles. Even more miraculous are the healings of mind, emotions, marital problems, etc. No one can ever say upon receiving the ministry of Spiritual Healing, *"Nothing happened."* Jesus is reaching out to bring to you the life abundant. This is your wholeness!

Worry and Spiritual Healing

Is there a cure for worry? This generation is trying to eliminate it. We are seeking to eliminate worry through insurance, social security, guaranteed annual wage, advances through medicine and technology, etc.

Yet, a recent survey revealed one out of five adults has or will have a nervous breakdown or serious nervous disorder.

The message of Spiritual Healing is that you can "*kick*" the worry habit.

NOT OF GOD

The plain and persistent teaching of Jesus is that we should not worry. He imparts the beautiful truth that our heavenly Father is tenderly caring for you. (Mt. 6:25-34)

Further, St. Paul assures you of the Lord's ability to meet your every need. (Phil. 4:19)

NEVER HELPS

Worry will not help your situation. In fact, worry is irrelevant to the solution to your real situation.

An analysis of worry in a large segment of our population revealed that —

1. 40% of an individual's worries were about past events or actions,

2. 50% of the worries concerned the future,

3. only 10% concerned current circumstances.

What a waste of energy! Great is the wisdom expressed in the statement, "*I never live with my yesterdays.*" It fits so well with Paul's statement, "*...forgetting the things which are behind...*" (Phil. 3:13)

The psalmist comforts us toward the future when he writes, "*My times are in Thy hands...*" (Ps. 31:15)

AFFIRM GOD'S PRESENCE

Affirming the Lord's presence will help you to replace the trivial with the important. It will lift your soul from the transient unto the eternal. It will enable you to concentrate upon the One who controls all instead of upon the things which seek to control you.

Wm. James has well said, "*The essence of genius is to know what to overlook.*" You should not overlook what the Lord has given you. "*For God has not given us the spirit of fear, but of power and of love, and of a sound mind.*" (II Tim. 1:7)

BE ACTIVE

Idleness is the devil's tool. Self-pity and withdrawal are often Satan's chosen instruments for furthering the worry habit. Kick the worry habit by actively seeking to do the following:

1. Deliberately discipline the mind to think on the Lord's promises.

2. Admit your weakness in the area of worry. Discuss this hang-up with a friend and together turn it over to the Lord and leave it with Him.

3. Regularly attend Spiritual Healing Services for help to keep your eyes upon the Problem Solver instead of upon your problems, (real or imagined) about which you worry.

4. Discover opportunities and become involved in areas of practical service. This may be community work, helping a school, changing vocations, going to work full or part-time, etc. Seek the Lord's wisdom and guidance concerning your involvement and follow Him.

5. Realistically face each situation which you encounter. If there is something you can do, seek wisdom as to how best to do it. Then do it!

If you can't do anything about the individual or situation because of distance, lack of ability, or other reasons, then put it in the Lord's hands and let it be there.

The prayer of serenity is worthy of your consideration and use.

"*God grant me the wisdom to accept the things I cannot change, courage to change the things I can, and wisdom to know the difference.*"

6. Don't worry about not worrying. You can "*kick*" the worry habit. Do so today! Amen.

You Are What You Think

Many Americans are weight conscious and carefully watch what they eat so as to maintain proper weight, or lose weight, or in some cases to gain. What we eat is important.

YOU ARE WHAT YOU THINK

You are what you think should be of greater concern to us than you are what you eat.

The real self is spiritual. The relationships to God and man are determined to a large extent by what you think. The Bible plainly teaches that your thoughts affect your entire life.

"Keep thy heart with all diligence; for out of it are the issues of life." (Pro. 4:23)

"For as he thinketh in his heart, so is he..." (Pro. 23:7)

"...Wherefore think ye evil in your hearts?" (Mt. 9:4)

THE HARD WAY

I learned the hard way that thoughts can affect one's health. They can have a bearing on your general well-being.

As a child of about eight I was at a family reunion. In my presence an uncle said to my father, *"Bill, Donald looks sick."*

Now, I felt fine, but this remark centered attention upon me. The thought flashed through my mind, *"Well, if I am ill I will be noticed. I will be an ill looking child to the best of my ability."*

A NEGATIVE PATTERN

My health was excellent until I was approximately 30 years old. Then this pattern of thought which had been more or less dormant from my childhood days began to bear fruit.

A serious illness had come upon me and I was getting progressively worse. Further, I saw nothing but more trouble for the future. This latent thought of desiring to be ill came to my conscious mind.

It was difficult for me to share with another believer that perhaps unconsciously I desired to be ill. However, I shared this with my wife and it meant a great deal to me. *You are what you think* had really come home to me. I had been unconsciously feeding wrong thoughts into my mind and body for many years. I was now reaping the harvest of something I didn't even realize I was doing.

THE POWER OF CONFESSION

The Lord used this confession to enable me to be delivered from the power of this evil thought. The power of the past had been broken.

I was grateful that He enabled me to replace the negative thought with the positive one of His desire for wholeness. Each of us needs to constantly believe that the Lord desires wholeness of body, mind, and spirit. Thanks be unto Him for the health I have enjoyed for many years.

WHOLENESS

In your mind are you convinced and willing to accept that the Lord desires wholeness for you?

Or are you often thinking, *"My situation or illness is too hard for the Lord."* The way you think deep within will have an effect upon your health and total well-being. The Apostle Paul knew the power of proper thinking when he wrote, *"Finally, brethren, whatsoever things are true...honest...just...pure...lovely...of good report, if there be any virtue, and if there be any praise, think on these things."* (Phil. 4:8)

A CLEAR CHANNEL

One who has been greatly used as a channel of healing has said, *"Any hurt bottled up within you will cause a condition that will get steadily worse until it is released. Worry, fear, anxiety and tenseness are all major causes of diseases that get beyond the power of science to make right."*

Beginning the Ministry of Healing

Many individuals have asked, *"How do you get started in the Spiritual Healing Ministry?"*

May I say there are as many ways as there are individuals and churches. However, there are some general guidelines which may be of help to you.

LAY THE FOUNDATION

A good foundation for the ministry of healing can be laid through the efforts of the pastor and lay individuals.

Tangible ways of doing this can include sermons about healing, reading books on healing, listening to cassette lectures by authorities in the ministry of healing, visiting healing services in other churches, offering a special course on healing during the Sunday School hour or other appropriate time, etc. All of these will enrich the lives of the participants.

INFORM THE CONGREGATION

There is no substitute for an informed official board and congregation concerning Spiritual Healing. The following is a sample letter which can be adapted to your situation. It will serve to inform the congregation of your decision to begin conducting public services of healing.

Dear Friends,

At a meeting May 3, official action was taken by (governing body) concerning involvement of our congregation in the Spiritual Healing Ministry. We want all to be fully aware of the importance and implications of this decision.

Whereas, Scripture directs us to call the elders of the Church when someone is sick to pray that they may be healed (James 5:14), and in -

- that we believe in the efficacy of prayer,

- that we believe God wills wholeness,

- that we believe all healing comes from God, whether it be through the various ministries of the church, medicines, physicians, or psychiatry,

- that we believe the root and intent of all healing prayer is establishing a right relationship with our Creator,

therefore, we the (governing body) of (your church name) authorize the Pastor to conduct Spiritual Healing Services on a regular basis.

We believe the Ministry of Spiritual Healing is based on the following four major premises. They are derived from our understanding of scripture.

1. That the primary purpose of the Spiritual Healing Ministry is to deepen a person's relationship with the living Christ. Physical and mental health are secondary to this primary concern.

2. That God wills wholeness for all His creation. The natural tendency of the body to "repair" itself, the demonstrated concern of Jesus for the total well-being of the people, and the promises of scripture confirm that God's will for us is wholeness.

3. That man is basically a unity. That is, in dealing with the needs of man, he must not be considered to be made up of soul, body, and spirit as if these were independent entities which can be dealt with in isolation.

What a person thinks influences how the body feels. The tone of spiritual health determines the state of one's emotions and mental outlook. How a person feels can affect spiritual vitality.

4. That a person's wholeness involves more than simply his/her own person. All relationships and attitudes toward others deeply influence your well-being. The soul, the body, the spirit, as well as the attitudes and relationships must be the foci of the healing ministry.

5. That positive, healing, reconciling, God-provided, spiritual forces are channeled into situations of need through the presence and prayers of God's people. Indeed, prayer is better understood as a "focusing" of spiritual power than as a verbalizing of requests to the Almighty.

We thank you for your prayer, participation, and helpful suggestions.

In the Name of the Great Physician,

*Signed*________________________________

(Pastor and/or Chair Person)

In conclusion, I stress that the core of any Spiritual Healing emphasis is the public healing service. It speaks to all of your faith and trust in God.

Resolution and Petition

There are often individuals in a congregation who are deeply interested in healing. They do feel the need of the church's healing ministry.

However, they sometimes feel neglected, misunderstood, and even rebuffed by their pastor and/or governing body.

GOVERNING BODY

The success of the Spiritual Healing Ministry cannot be attained through the pastor's leading alone. Neither will success be achieved through the enthusiastic endorsement of one or two of the local congregation.

The healing ministry must have the endorsement and support of the governing body of the congregation. This endorsement must be more than simply passing a motion that there will be healing services.

The strongest endorsement which the governing body can give is the participation of those who serve on this board. Their presence at the healing services and other activities pertaining to the healing emphasis will speak far louder than any motion they could ever pass.

Frequently the governing body assumes the position of merely passing on suggestions or endorsing programs, but members never support their actions with their participation.

Your congregation does not need more resolutions or decisions concerning the rightness, wrongness, or appropriateness of some program or activity. Congregations today need leaders who will lead; individuals who will, by example, support their program suggestions.

A RESOLUTION

An *"Indication of Interest"* Resolution and Petition will often help the governing body to endorse a ministry of healing . It will serve to bridge the differences and remove hindrances to beginning a healing emphasis.

PROPER SPIRIT

The Resolution and Petition should never be presented in the spirit of simply trying to prove a point or to coerce. It is a tangible effort to indicate the interest within the congregation concerning the healing ministry. It serves as a catalyst for the pastor and governing body to consider the need and situation.

The following Resolution and Petition may be adapted to your situation.

WHEREAS, *the ministry of Jesus Christ was one of preaching, teaching, and healing, and —*

WHEREAS, *He gave the power to heal, first to His 12 disciples, then later to other seventy, —*

WHEREAS, *He commissioned His Church, His Living Body on earth for all time to preach, teach and heal, —*

WHEREAS, *the early Apostolic Church obeyed this Divine Commission and through their obedience they exhibited great power, —*

WHEREAS, *we believe that the Divine Commission was intended for all generations, including ours, —*

WHEREAS, *there is great need for Spiritual Healing in our day, and many denominations endorse this ministry and countless congregations of practically all denominations now hold services of healing of body and soul as well as spirit, —*

WHEREAS, a number of members of our congregation are willing to become involved in and to support such a ministry, —

THEREFORE,

We petition our (name of governing body) to more fully emphasize the Spiritual Healing Ministry and to schedule and conduct Spiritual Healing Services as an integral part of the total ministry of our congregation.

We, the undersigned, pledge that with God's help we will support the Spiritual Healing Ministry and the healing services through our prayers, attendance, and finances.

COOPERATION

Those signing the above Resolution and Petition should always strive to work very carefully with the Governing Body. Cooperation is essential to the wholeness you desire.

Christian Science and Unity

What is the relationship of Spiritual Healing to Christian Science and Unity?

I present below pages 41 and 42 of the report adopted by the 172nd General Assembly of the United Presbyterian Church, USA in 1960. It is one of the best statements I have read concerning Christian Science and Unity in relationship to the Christian faith.

CHRISTIAN SCIENCE

"Christian Science is the most explicit and absolute of the religious movements emphasizing the connection between faith and health. It is the contention of Christian Science that reality is pure spirit. Matter is regarded as non-existent — a misconception of reality. The pain and death connected with matter is therefore also non-existent, the remedy is knowledge of God, who is conceived as pure spirit. Adequate knowledge of God banishes pain and death because such knowledge understands their *"material"* or illusory character. In practice Christian Science seeks to correct the thinking of believers by instructing them out of the Bible according to *Science and Health with Key to the Scriptures,* the official interpretation of the Bible by the founder, Mary Baker Eddy, and by devotional exercises. Resort to physicians or members of allied professions is tolerated to the extent that the individual believer has not yet achieved the ideal detachment from the material world which Christian Science strives to effect.

QUESTION OF TRUTH

"The concerns of the Church regarding Christian Science are two-fold. One concern is the question of truth. There are fundamental doctrines of this faith which cannot be reconciled with the truth as it comes to us in Christ. These include basic beliefs about which there are serious differences of interpretation: The goodness of the material creation, the reality of sin, the Incarnation of God in Christ and the Cross of Calvary as the atonement for our sins. As a matter of fact, Christian Scientists believe that their movement is the authoritative interpreter of Christ to the world.

EFFECTS UPON PERSONS

"The other concern is the effects upon persons. Not only does the Christian Science movement tend to dissuade people from making use of care which physicians and other members of the physical and mental health team can provide as a result of modern science, but a far more serious effect is to encourage the belief that no type of evil exists in the world except ignorance.

"This position, seriously promulgated, undercuts the spiritual support that is needed for the further advancement of medical research and medical practice, which we regard as a major Christian contribution to the prevention of illness and the cure of disease. Fortunately Christian Science in practice has sometimes been more relevant than its theory. Insofar as it helps man to recognize the reality of certain Christian virtues such as love, the relevance of faith in God to mental and physical health and the sovereignty of God over all of mortal life, it is setting forth elements of Christian truth which the Church should proclaim in every generation.

UNITY

"The Unity School of Christianity was founded by the Charles Fillmores. It is a variation of the same school of thought but with certain Hindu features added, such as the idea of reincarnation. The emphasis of Unity is upon the identification with God which the believer already possesses, if he would only recognize it. Man is encouraged to think of himself as endowed with the *'I am'* power of God. All forms of finiteness, including sin, disease and death, can be overcome by asserting the power of the immortal soul over matter. The same concerns the Church has about Christian Science she has about Unity.

"Christian Science and Unity...call the Church to re-examine its promulgation of the Gospel with a view to assessing the completeness of her witness. Certainly one of the factors which has contributed to the rise of such movements is the ignoring of relationships between faith and health by the Churches."

The Occult and Spiritual Healing

Millions throughout the world are pursuing the occult. They are seeking an answer to the problems of our day and feel that there is an easy answer.

Witchcraft and other forms of the occult are often a part of even the highly educated person's experiences. Witchcraft is even penetrating the sports field.

For instance, the records of a Kenya soccer club revealed an annual expense item of $3,600.00 for witchcraft.

It is reported that other clubs also employ witch-doctors for consultation on strategy and chances of winning. They refuse to announce names of players in advance lest they be bewitched. Before vital games they have sentries patrolling the stadium to see that no one places a charm on the ball.

WITCHES

It is reported that England now has at least 30,000 practicing witches. We know that in the United States the stampede to the occult is staggering.

One is led to ask of our modern day, *"Is this the age of enlightenment or of darkness?"*

OCCULT

The dictionary defines *"occult"* as beyond the bounds of ordinary knowledge, secret, involving the alleged knowledge or employment of secret or mysterious agencies. Falling into this category from the Christian viewpoint would be: fortune-telling, magic practices, religious cults, spiritism, ouija boards, horoscopes, clairvoyance, and witchcraft.

SCRIPTURE

The Scriptures do not deny the power of the occult, but rather denounce the occult.

The following reference is significant. *"There shall not be found with thee any one...that useth divination* (fortune-telling), *or an observer of times* (soothsayer), *or a consulter with familiar spirits* (medium), *or an enchanter* (magician), *or a witch* (sorceress), *or a charmer* (hypnotist), *or a necromancer* (medium who consults the dead). *For all that do these things are an abomination unto the Lord..."* (Deut. 18:10-12)

Do you need further admonition? If so, please consider the following Scriptures. (Lev. 19:31; 20-27; 19:26; Ex 22:18; I Sam. 28:3; II Kings 21:5-8; II Chr. 33:5-9; Isa. 2:6; Jer. 27:8-11; Zech. 10:2; Mal. 3:5; Acts 8:4-25; 16:16-24; 19:11-20; I Tim. 4:1; Rev. 21:8; 22:15.)

The prophet thunders, *"And when they say to you, consult the mediums and the wizards who chirp and mutter, should not a people consult their God? Should they consult the dead on behalf of the living?"* (Isa. 8:19)

GOD'S POWER

The occult may imitate God's power (Ex. 7:11-13; Acts 8:11) but can never impart it. The power to become sons of God is only from Jesus Christ. (John 1:12,13) You can combat the forces and false teachings of the occult through the whole armor of God. (Eph. 6:10-20) Jesus Christ is the only answer and only Mediator in our day as in all days. (John 14:6)

THE EARLY CHURCH

The early Church had little patience with the spirit, which was contrary to the Spirit of the Living God. Simon the sorcerer was commanded to repent for his wickedness. (Acts 8:22) The spirit of divination in the slave girl was rebuked. (Acts 16:18)

Fourteen Tenets

There are basic tenets of the healing ministry which serve as a foundation of our efforts.

The following fourteen will give you a better understanding of the approach and aims of Spiritual Healing.

I. ALL OF GOD

We believe that all healing is of God.

II. DESIRES WHOLENESS

We believe that God desires for us wholeness and health. Jesus spent much of His time here on earth healing the sick and He came to always do the Father's will.

III. MANY AGENCIES

We believe that God uses many agencies for healing. These include medicine, surgery, psychiatry, physician, prayer, confession, etc.

IV. HUMAN CHANNELS

We believe that God works almost invariably through human channels to do His healing. We are to be willing channels to do His Will.

V. NOT MAGIC

We believe that Spiritual Healing is not magic, hocus-pocus or sleight-of-hand. It is simply taking God at His word. In faith, believing, you make intercession for healing and thank Him for what is already taking place.

VI. WITHIN THE CHURCH

We believe that God's healing power operates within the Church which is the Body of Christ here on earth, but it is not limited to His Church.

VII. RIGHTEOUSNESS

We believe that physical health does not necessarily indicate righteousness nor does illness necessarily indicate specific sins in a person's life.

VIII. PROMOTE HEALTH

We believe that Christian witness and fellowship promote health and in many ways prevent illness by providing purposeful living and wholesome companionship. This results in proper stewardship of strength and health.

IX. CHRIST'S MINISTRY

We believe that healing was an important part of Christ's ministry here on earth and is intended to be a part of His disciples' work in every generation.

X. NO FAILURES

We believe that there are no failures in Spiritual Healing. No one can be brought into the presence of the healing Christ without being changed spiritually, emotionally, or physically. In some cases they are changed in all three areas.

XI. CHRIST LIVES

We believe that Jesus Christ lives today in His risen power. He is the same today as yesterday and will be the same forever and ever.

XII. SALVATION

We believe that the word *salvation* means not only deliverance from sin and death, but also deliverance from physical and mental evils.

XIII. REVIVAL

We believe that the revival of Spiritual Healing in the Church today may be the means of the greatest advance in Christianity in this century.

XIV. BELIEVE

We believe that what we believe is vital for both our present and our future.

In conclusion I present the question to you. *What do you believe?*

Some Benefits of a Spiritual Healing Ministry

Are there benefits derived from a healing ministry? What are some valid reasons for the emphasis upon the Lord's desire for wholeness?

CONCERN

The ministry of healing helps to develop a fellowship of concern. It helps bring a fellowship of the concerned.

It is so easy for an individual to be lost in the complexity of modern church life. Especially the healing services provide opportunity for the concerned to focus their prayers, affection, and love upon particular individuals. It is in such services that joy, sorrows, victories, defeats, and concerns become shared experiences. There comes the realization that what happens to one, in a sense, happens to all.

REALITY

Another benefit of the ministry of healing is that it helps believers to be aware of the reality of His Presence. Our Lord is seen as being very near. His love is real. His concern is genuine. His power is present. His desire is wholeness.

Many testify that during the healing service they feel His presence and power as at no other time. *"Lo, I am with you always,"* is not simply a statement, but stark reality.

WHERE THE ACTION IS

The healing service is not simply another hour of theory and theology. Action is the keynote of it. People are praying and believing and when they do something happens. Prayer is power. It does change you and others.

There may not always be phenomenal physical recovery, but there is always a deepening of the spiritual life, a gaining of insight, or recovery of strength. As the old saying goes, *"The healing service is where the saw meets the wood."*

A change is inevitable in both the ones ministering and the ones ministered unto.

FIRST THINGS FIRST

The healing ministry brings a natural increase of interest in prayer. It helps individuals to realize that prayer is not to equip you to do the work of the Church, but that prayer is the work of the Church.

Jesus said, *"Men ought always to pray and not to faint."* (Luke 18:1) The viewpoint of most Christians today is that Jesus said, *"You ought always to organize, plan, and promote; and be busy beavers."*

The ministry of healing will teach you to wait upon the Lord and to trust in His power.

INDIVIDUAL PARTICIPATION

People at the healing service do not remain passive in the pews. They are participants. Each has the opportunity to receive the Laying-on-of-Hands with prayer. They bring to the altar their concerns and the concerns they have for others.

Even if you choose to remain in your pew through the entire service there is still a deep personal concern you feel for others.

In a sense, each one present is a channel of power.

THE WHOLE PERSON

Another benefit of the healing ministry is that it gives opportunity to express the basic belief of the close relationship of the physical, spiritual, emotional aspects of a person.

The Church is called to minister to the whole person. The ministry of healing offers the most balanced approach I know to the total needs of each person.

PREVENTION OF ILLNESS

The healing ministry provides guidance for a person to appropriate the strength to remain strong of body, soul, and spirit. It even helps to develop one's personality to the place where you can better cope with illness and other problems. Preventive medicine is in vogue today and includes trusting God.

How to Receive God's Blessing

Each one of us is most anxious to receive all the Lord has in store for us. How can this best be done? May I offer the following suggestions.

I. SEEK GUIDANCE

Invite the Holy Spirit to guide you as you begin to prepare yourself to receive God's best. He may give you a Bible passage or message, a person or an experience as part of the answer and comfort for your need.

"Likewise the Spirit also helpeth our infirmities: for we know not what we should pray for as we ought: but the Spirit itself maketh intercession for us with groanings which cannot be uttered." (Romans 8:26)

II. GIVE THANKS

Give thanks to God for what He has already done for you and your loved ones. Thank God for what the one in need has already meant to you. Count your many blessings.

"Be careful for nothing. But in every thing by prayer and supplication with thanksgiving let your requests be made known unto God." (Phil. 4:6)

III. FORGIVE

Forgive everyone who has injured you in any way. Do all you can to be at peace with all. Even be willing to ask those you have injured to forgive you.

"And when you stand praying, forgive, if ye have ought against any that your Father also which is in heaven may forgive you your trespasses." (Mark 11:25)

IV. DETERMINE NEED

Seek to agree in yourself and with your family what is most needed at the time and why it is needed.

"Again I say unto you, That if two of you shall agree on earth as touching anything that they shall ask, it shall be done for them of my Father which is in heaven." (Mt. 18:19)

V. RELINQUISHMENT

Relinquish your life into God's hands. Let Him make His improvements in you. Be willing to exchange what you think is best for yourself for His best for you.

"And no man putteth new wine into old bottles; else the new wine will burst the bottles, and be spilled, and the bottles shall perish." (Luke 5:37)

VI. OPEN TO GOD

Invite Jesus to come within you and support you while you are waiting for God's best. As a flower opens to receive light, rain, and air; may you open yourself to receive God's best.

"Behold, I stand at the door, and knock: if any man hear my voice and open the door, I will come in to him, and will sup with him, and he with me." (Rev. 3:20)

VII. PICTURE THE BEST

I encourage you to make a picture in your mind of God's best coming to you.

"For as he thinketh in his heart, so is he. Eat and drink, saith he to thee, but his heart is not with thee." (Pro. 23:7)

VIII. EXPECT THE BEST

Seek to begin each day thinking of what good thing the Lord has in store for you. Expect the Lord to bless. Do not dwell on the dreaded areas of your life, but on the blessed areas.

"Therefore I say unto you, What things soever ye desire, when ye pray believe that ye receive them, and ye shall have them." (Mk. 11:24)

IX. REST IN GOD

Learn to abide in His care. Rest yourself and your loved ones in the security of God's love which was with you when you were born, which is with you now, and which will be with you through all eternity.

"If ye abide in me, and my words abide in you, ye shall ask what ye will, and it shall be done unto you." (John 15:7)

X. TURN TO GOD

Seek to always keep your heart and life turned in the Lord's direction. Prayer is the process by which you get yourself into alignment with the Lord to receive His best. Regardless of your circumstances return unto the Father.

"I will arise and go to my father, and will say unto him, Father I have sinned against heaven, and before thee." (Luke 15:18)

XI. RELATE

Relate to what God has done for you in the past which is *faith*. Relate to what He is going to do for you in the future which is *hope*. Relate to what He is doing for you now which is *love*.

"And now abideth faith, hope, love, these three; but the greatest of these is love." (I Cor. 13:13)

A Matter of Devotion

I am often asked why I am so devoted to the ministry of healing. My response to this valid question is always the same.

"I am not devoted to the healing ministry. I am devoted to Jesus Christ."

DYNAMITE OF OBEDIENCE

I am not devoted to some program or to a plan. I am devoted to a Person. That Person is Jesus Christ.

My calling is not to meet some need in the world. I have been called to do the will of the Creator of the world. Doing His will issues forth the dynamite of obedience.

My pastoral ministry and that of any pastor is enriched by accepting all that Jesus has in store for His people. It is not that healing is my *"bag,"* but rather that Jesus is my Lord.

I am called to be a pastor of a local congregation. If I am faithful to my calling the Lord's message of wholeness will be my message. My ministry is not an emphasis upon healing so much as it is endeavoring to lift up our Lord in my parish. Healings are the natural result of obedience to our Lord. It is tangibly beholding His presence and power.

SUMMARY OF CHRIST'S MINSTRY

There are two places in the Bible where our Lord's ministry is presented in capsule form. Both instances present healing as a vital aspect of His ministry.

The first is when the disciples of John the Baptist ask Christ if He is truly the Messiah or should they look for someone else. Jesus replied by having them tell John what He was doing and what they had actually seen.

"...Go and show John again those things which ye do hear and see: The blind receive their sight, and the lame walk, the lepers are cleansed, and the deaf hear, the dead are raised up, and the poor have the gospel preached to them..." (Mt. 11:2-6)

The second reference is Peter's summary of the ministry of Jesus. He is preaching to the Gentiles and wants them to understand the ministry of our Lord.

"How God anointed Jesus of Nazareth with the Holy Ghost and with power; who went about doing good, and healing all that were oppresed of the devil; for God was with Him." (Acts 10:38)

DEVOTION TO CHRIST

I want to present some reasons why devotion to Christ will lead to a ministry of healing. I feel they are worthy of your careful and prayerful consideration.

1. The very nature of Christ is a spirit of compassion. He desired wholeness for the afflicted and the oppressed. His very nature lead Him to be constantly ministering to individuals in all areas of their life. He did not hesitate to bring healing to them.

2. Jesus' commission to His disciples included healing. They were to proclaim that the Kingdom of God was at hand, and they were to heal the sick.

His disciples were told to believe Jesus wanted the sick well and to tell the sick the Good News of wholeness. See Mt. 10:1; Mark 6:7-13; Luke 9:1-6.

3. The early church leaders believed the Lord desired wholeness. The disciples did not proclaim or develop a program. They presented a Person, Jesus Christ.

A natural result of lifting up the Lord Jesus were the *"signs and wonders."* These were the proof of the full gospel being faithfully proclaimed. See Rom. 15:18-19; Heb. 2:4; II Cor. 12:12. The real question is not why a healing ministry, but why not a healing ministry?

Proclaim All of the Good News

The Christian faith has many facets such as teaching, preaching, prayer, social concern, healing, etc.

Is it not strange, however, that traditionally the healing aspect has been so sorely neglected? It comprised such a large part of our Lord's ministry and that of the Apostolic Church. I am amazed at its neglect by the Institutional Church through the centuries.

IN A NUTSHELL

Peter capsuled our Lord's ministry in this fashion. *"Now God anointed Jesus of Nazareth with the Holy Ghost and with power: who went about doing good, and Healing all that were oppressed by the devil, for God was with Him '* (Acts 10:38)

These words certainly put our Lord's ministry in a nutshell. They tell it like it is.

VINDICATION

It is noteworthy how Jesus vindicated His own ministry. John's disciples were sent to inquire if He be the Christ or should they be looking for another One.

Jesus did not give them a detailed theological message nor a philosophical discourse. He said, *"Go and shew John again those things which ye do hear and see; the blind receive their sight, and the lame walk, the lepers are cleansed, and the deaf hear, the dead are raised up, and the poor have the gospel preached to them."* (Mt. 11:4,5)

TRUTH DEMONSTRATED

Jesus did not merely declare that the Kingdom of God is at hand. He demonstrated this truth. His miracles were evidence of the presence of God.

Even Nicodemus was reached through the healing ministry of our Lord. He was attracted by the miracles of our Lord. *"...no man can do these miracles that thou doest, except God be with him."* (John 3:2)

HARMONY OF THE GOSPELS

A harmony of the Gospels reveals the startling fact that approximately one out of every three incidents in the life of our Lord concerns healing.

From the beginning of His public ministry to His last hours He worked miracles of healing.

If so much of His ministry was that of helping others through healing, how can we neglect this message of hope?

POWER AVAILABLE

Centuries of neglect does not negate the fact that the power of Jesus Christ is available. Niagara Falls has existed for eons, but it was not until recently that its great power was harnessed for the good of mankind.

Most Christians have sought to convert the unbeliever and to edify the believer through proper theology. Yet, it is evident that a congregation is not presenting a complete ministry if healing is neglected.

Biblical preaching, prayer, sacraments, evangelism, etc. cannot be be substituted for the power of the Gospel. The evidence of the power is to see His miracles in our day.

PRECEDENT

The precedent for imparting wholeness was set by our Lord. (Acts 10:38) The power is available. (Mt. 28:18; John 14:12-14) The procedure is simply believing the Lord for great and marvelous things. (Mt. 17:20,21)

PREACH ALL

Every Christian and every Christian congregation is called to the whole person. This must include the proclamation and appropriation of our Lord's healing power. The Great Physician is for our day! You and I are called to proclaim all of the Good News, not just selected portions of it.

A Symbol of Healing

This Symbol of Healing is an effort on my part to visually convey the message of healing.

I feel the Lord revealed to me the insights concerning the Symbol and my daughter-in-law, Patrice Bartow, did the art work.

The Symbol imparts the concept that the Triune God is the agent of healing. Also that it is by faith that we receive and impart the blessings and message of healing.

It is my prayer that the Symbol of Healing will help implant upon your mind and heart the essential aspects of the Spiritual Healing Ministry. May you believe and receive the Lord's wholeness for you and yours.

The following is my interpretation of the Symbol of Healing. You may have other insights as you observe the Symbol in the light of what I have written.

THE CIRCLE

The circle of the Symbol represents God the Father. He is over all and desirous of extending His healing, love, and mercy to all. His very nature is such that He seeks to extend His wholeness to us.

He is more willing to heal than we are often willing to accept His healings. See: Ps. 34:8; 40:5; 86:15; Mt. 5:45; Lu. 11:13; I Pet. 5:7.

THE SHIELD

The shield of the Symbol represents Faith. It is the gift of God and so vital for an effective ministry of healing.

Because of my effort to teach that faith is a gift from God the shield is touching the circle and is being presented to you by the hands of the Lord Jesus. See: Eph. 2:8,9; Lu. 17:5; Gal. 5:6; Ja. 2:17; I Jo. 5:4.

THE HANDS

The hands holding and offering the Shield of Faith represent the hands of the Lord Jesus Christ. He is giving to you the faith to believe that He desires the very best for you. The hands speak of the truth that the Lord completely identified Himself with humanity and continues to do so. See: Lu. 2:11; Mt. 25:40; Acts 9:4; 10:38; Phil. 2:5-8.

THE DOVE

The dove of the Symbol represents the Holy Spirit. The healing gift, message, and ministry are of divine origin and power.

It is the Holy Spirit Who enables you to behold the love and mystery of the Lord's tender care. See: Lu. 11:13; 24:29; Acts 1:8; Rom. 8:11; Jo. 16:13; 14:17.

THE HAND

The hand on the shield represents the one ministering. The hand is used to bestow a blessing upon the one for whom prayer is being offered. The hand issues forth from the hand of the Lord Jesus. It is touched by the dove which is symbolic of the power of the Holy Spirit working through the individual.

The hand is on the shield of faith and thus speaks of this vital ingredient. The shield is touching the circle which represents the Father. Thus the blessing is imparted in the Name of God the Father, Son, and Holy Spirit.

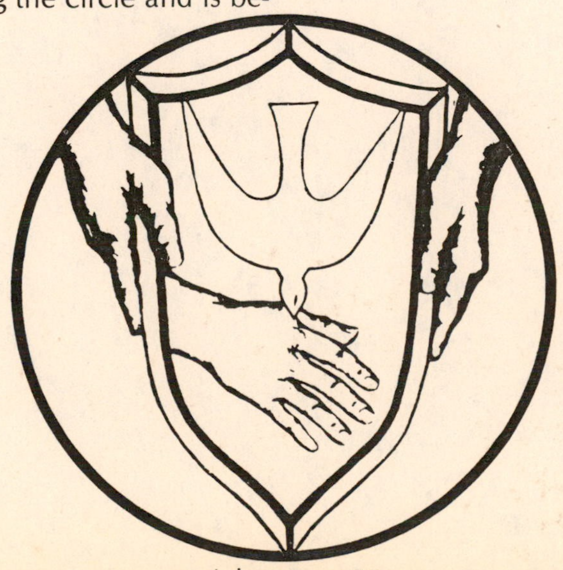

Fear — Obstacle To Healing

It is my firm conviction that every believer and every congregation would be blessed beyond measure if they would accept what the Lord has in store for them.

If this be true then a very fair question is, *"Why do so many people neglect the things of the Lord?"*

Another important question is, *"Why is healing from the Lord shunned by so many people?"*

OBSTACLES TO HEALING

Many individuals neglect the healing ministry because they cannot surmount the apparent obstacles.

There are several common obstacles which effectively block the power of the Lord in an individual's life. They will also prove a stumbling block to the healing ministry of a congregation.

THE UNKNOWN

The first obstacle I mention is false fear. Many people are left powerless with unwarranted fears. One of these unwarranted fears in the healing ministry arises from the fear of the unknown.

Many feel that all healing of the body should be in the hands of the medical doctor. The ills of the mind left to the psychiatrist.

They fail to appreciate these persons of science are instruments of God's healing. They do not understand the living, present, power of Christ.

A WELL CHARTED COURSE

You need to realize that involvement in the ministry of healing is not a step into the unknown.

In fact, it is pursuing the teachings of our Lord and the efforts of the devoted through the centuries.

If you are hesitant because of the fear of the unknown, please consider the following:

1. There are many healings recorded in the Gospels. Jesus Christ who healed then is *"...the same yesterday, today, and forever."* (Heb. 13:8)

2. The history of the early Church, the Book of Acts, contains many instances of healing. (Acts. 3:6-8)

3. During the first three centuries of the Church healing miracles were common experiences. It was not until the Church became *"popular"* that it became *"powerless."*

4. Throughout the centuries there have been many individuals greatly used of the Lord in a ministry of healing.

Through the ages those willing to believe the Bible means what it says have been channels of God's healing power.

5. Hundreds of congregations are today witnessing a new power from God. The healing ministry is being discovered as very much a part of the total ministry of a local congregation.

6. There now exist many wonderful books in the area of healing. More are being produced all the time.

All of the above witness to the fact that we do not have to travel in the land of fear of the unknown.

The course has been well-charted for you. There is abundant proof of God's desire for your wholeness. There is abundant proof that His Church should be a healing Church.

Fear of the unknown is a false fear. Cast it aside. Do not permit it to hinder you from exercising great faith in the Lord's healing power. He can and will heal!

Fear — Obstacle to Healing

Fear is always lurking its ugly head to discourage Christians. This is especially true in the area of healing.

FEAR OF OTHERS

One of the fears hindering the healing ministry is, *"What will others think if I become involved in the ministry of healing?"*

Many Christians have been *"brainwashed"* to the point of thinking they must please others instead of God. The early Christians had to make a decision as to whom they would serve. (Acts 4:19) You must do likewise. Jesus said that we are called to fear only the living God. (Mt. 10:28)

Believers cannot wait until all have accepted the healing message before proclaiming Jesus Christ as the Great Physician. In fact, only a few in any one congregation may really believe this. However, the church has always moved forward on the faithfulness of the remnant.

NOT YET READY

Pastors and lay persons often say, *"But our congregation is not ready for the message of healing."* My answer is that everyone in the congregation will never be ready. The few who are ready need to be encouraged and used as channels of healing.

Think for a moment! How many of your congregation are ready for tithing? What if you were to suggest that there be no more contributions made to your church until every member agreed to tithe? You say, *"How ridiculous!"* Yes, but is not that the same logic we use when we neglect to emphasize the message of healing because some may not understand or are unwilling to accept it?

Cease to fear others and go on for God with the ministry of healing as a part of your congregational life.

WHAT WILL THEY THINK

Another fear is, *"What will others think when I tell them Christ can heal and I am afflicted myself?"* Satan used this fear on me for a long time.

It was in 1959 that I felt led to begin public services of healing. At the time I was gravely ill. My legs were wrapped in elastic stockings each morning to help keep them from swelling throughout the day. I could not turn over in bed without hooking one leg over the edge of the bed to help pull me over. I was in constant pain and very weak. It was in this afflicted state that the Lord led me to begin the healing services.

After holding the services for a few months Satan attacked by saying, *"How can you lay-on-hands for others to be healed when you are so ill yourself?"*

This almost defeated me. I am grateful that the Holy Spirit came to my rescue at that moment. He asked, *"Do you proclaim a perfect plan of salvation?"* My instant reply was *"yes."* He asked, *"Are you perfect?"* My reply, *"No!" Christ alone is perfect. It is He I proclaim."*

It was then that I clearly saw the truth. The healing message is not dependent upon my good or bad health. It is like the message of salvation which is not dependent upon my perfection. Christ is the Healer. I was called to be the proclaimer, not the explainer.

Now I was able to rebuke the inward fear and tell the Lord, *"I will hold healing services until the day I die even if I must do so from a wheel chair."* I hasten to say that a funny thing happened on the way to the wheel chair. I was marvelously healed.

HEALED IN SPIRIT

Emily Gardner Neal in her book, *"The Healing Power of Christ,"* beautifully writes of her call to the ministry of healing in spite of continued physical affliction. She tells what her affliction has taught her. *"I was to learn what it was to be stripped of pride, ...I was to learn patience, ...I was to learn a new compassion for all who suffer, ...I was to learn through experience the validity of what I have so long taught..."*

Misunderstanding — Obstacle to Healing

Misunderstanding as to the nature and place of Spiritual Healing is one of the greatest obstacles facing this ministry. If this obstacle is to be overcome, much effort is needed to interest and to inform individuals and local congregations. I offer the following as steps toward removing the obstacle of misunderstanding.

SERMONS

The pastor sets the pace for this vital ministry. A series of messages can introduce and explain Spiritual Healing to the congregation and occasional messages can keep them current on the subject.

MISSIONS AND CONFERENCES

Individuals interested in Spiritual Healing should be encouraged to attend Missions and Conferences on Spiritual Healing. The local congregation should assume all or part of the expense of those delegated to attend. It is especially important that the pastor attend such activities. He needs to be informed and inspired.

VISITING SERVICES

There are always new ideas, insights, and enthusiasm to be gained through attendance at a service elsewhere. This is a good way to introduce individuals to the need and possibilities of such a service in your own parish.

HEALING SUNDAY

Most churches have all kinds of special Sundays throughout the year. What is more important than one which emphasizes Spiritual Healing? Illness and problems are common to all individuals and families. They need guidance how to best meet their problems. Guest speakers, informed Sunday School teachers, lay witnesses, can all help make this Sunday most valuable.

ARTICLES

The parish letter, Sunday bulletin, or monthly newsletter are channels of information. The pastor or lay member of the congregation can write concerning healing.The Adventures in this book may be copied and used in any way most helpful to you and your congregation.

READING

Spiritual Healing materials should be in an easily accessible place. Periodically attention should be called to good books, magazines, and other resources which will help individuals understand the message of healing. A spiritual healing library can be developed over a period of time.

CLASSES

Many Sunday Schools have presented a course in the area of Spiritual Healing. Some have used guest leaders for these courses. Many communities have had Spiritual Healing as one of the courses in their united School of Religion. Six to thirteen weeks can easily be devoted to this vital topic.

ENDORSEMENT

The success of Spiritual Healing cannot be attained simply through the pastor's leading, or through enthusiastic endorsement by one or two lay people. It must have the endorsement and support of the local governing group. Congregations today need leaders who will be examples that say Spiritual Healing is important. It is not an option for you and for me. We can overcome every obstacle.

Resentment — Obstacle to Healing

Resentment is one of the biggest obstacles to healing that I know. There are literally thousands of Christians suffering the consequences of resentment toward their spouse, relative, pastor, church, business associate, neighbor, or other situation or person.

It is impossible to estimate the stomach trouble, emotional problems, and other physical ailments resulting from these resentments.

OBSTACLE

There are many reasons why resentment is an obstacle to healing. I list a few of them.

1. It blocks the channel of God's forgiving spirit in your life.
2. It brings a haze across your life which throws all individuals and situations out of focus. Resentment will tarnish all of your situations and decisions.
3. It continually pours the poisons of negative and destructive thinking into your body, soul, and spirit.

It is no figment of the imagination when someone says, *"He gives me a pain in the neck."* The bitter fruit of resentment is often manifest in the physical body. This is vividly illustrated by the individual who told the guest-speaker that during his message he resolved a long-standing resentment toward his mother. The exciting thing to him was that the moment he had resolved the resentment in his heart he lost the pain in his neck and shoulders. This pain he had endured for years in spite of an abundance of medical treatment for it.

GUIDELINES

I would like to present some practical guidelines for removing resentment.

I. PRACTICE THE PRESENCE

I strongly encourage you to seek to constantly practice the presence of the Lord. The use of devotional literature, moments of silence, confession, worship, etc. will all help you. The following Bible verses are worth your careful consideration. Mark 11:25; Luke 17:4; Eph. 4:32; Col. 3:13.

II. SINCERELY PRAY

Resentment can be helped a great deal by sincerely praying for the one you resent. Pray for specific blessings for the person. Lift the individual to the throne of Grace. Consider all aspects of the person or situation which are annoying you and commit them unto the Lord.

III. THE LORD'S PRAYER

I suggest that you frequently pray the Lord's Prayer. Especially open your life to the portion which says, *"Forgive me my trespasses as I forgive ______ ______."* Actually say the name of the one or ones you resent.

IV. LEARN FORBEARANCE

Each of us falls far short of perfection. Wm. Cowper spoke to all when he wrote:

"The kindest and the happiest pair
Will find occasion to forbear;
And something, every day they live,
To pity, and perhaps forgive."

V. BE REAL

Realize the *"real"* person is one who does not harbor *"little"* or or *"big"* resentments. There is no virtue in defending yourself and saying, *"I'll never forgive."* This only produces more stress.

VI. FORGIVE NOW

Plans to someday forgive are not enough. You must be willing to forgive now. At least be willing to let the Lord help you over your resentment.

VII. SPEAK KINDLY

You need not continue to speak ill of the one you resent. Kind words will serve to reduce harsh feelings within your heart.

VIII. TANGIBLE ACTION

The Lord may direct you to write a letter, confess to a person, make restitution, or have a heart to heart talk as a tangible act to forgive. Remove the obstacle of resentment today! It can be done. Do it now!

Emotionally Induced Wholeness

The letters E. I. I. are often used to signify *Emotionally Induced Illnesses.* Many hospital beds are occupied by individuals who have *"thought"* themselves into a state of illness. In addition, many illnesses could have been prevented if individuals had a proper approach to life.

It is not difficult for me to convince individuals that illness is often emotionally induced. Most people are aware of problems of their own or others which are the result of wrong mental and emotional attitudes.

E.I.W.

I want you to consider what I term E. I. W. which stands for *Emotionally Induced Wholeness.*

The Lord desires your wholeness. It is important you believe this and trust Him for it.

Your mental attitude can help maintain wholeness and help restore it when illness does happen to come your way.

STEPS TO E.I.W.

I suggest the following tangible ways to help with your *Emotionally Induced Wholeness.*

1. Discipline yourself to begin each day visualizing yourself as whole. Use your God given power of imagination to visualize the Lord Jesus being with you. See Him extending His wholeness to every aspect of your body, soul, and spirit.

Endeavor to repeat this procedure at least three times throughout the day. Often repeat the words of Jesus, *"...what things ye desire, when ye pray, believe that ye receive them, and ye shall have them."* (Mark 11:24)

2. If you have developed any type of illness visualize yourself as whole. It doesn't matter if it be a specific organ of the body or simply a general illness. Visualize the healing power of the Lord flowing into the affected area and bringing wholeness.

C. S. Lovett suggests visualizing wholeness and applying the Lord's healing laws by:

a. "Seeing the organ (or whatever part is affected) as completely healed and in a perfect state — and thanking Him for it."

b. "Seeing yourself doing things which you would normally do if you did not have the affliction."

3. Visualize yourself as in the perfect light and love of the Lord. This permits you to get your mind off of the problem and unto the Problem Solver. It keeps you from dwelling upon the affliction and inadequacy of yourself. It leads to concentration upon the Great Physician and His all sufficiency.

Dwelling upon your pain or illness simply drives it deeper into the recesses of your mind and total being. Looking unto the Great Physician focuses power and attention at the proper place.

4. When you pray for others visualize them in the light and love of Jesus. Ask the one for whom you are praying to visualize himself in His light and love.

AS YOU BELIEVE

Dr. Carl Simonton conducted experiments on 152 patients he was treating with cobalt radiation. He instructed each patient to visualize what the cobalt was doing to the cancer. They were to picture the cancerous area as raw hamburger or raw liver with a vast army of millions of tiny white blood cells attacking the cancer cells and carrying them away.

The 20 patients who really applied his directions for visualizing wholeness were the only ones whose response to radiation was rated *"excellent."*

The 63 patients who were *"good"* in response to visualizing wholeness achieved *"good"* results from radiation. Those who were indifferent to blending the visualizing of wholeness with radiation treatment had only *"fair"* or *"poor"* results.

Dr. Simonton says, *"I strongly believe that health is influenced by a patient's mental attitude."* His conclusion is not new. Jesus believed in the power of believing.

Victory Over Nervous Disorders

Nervous disorders have reached epidemic proportions in our nation. It is estimated that at least one of every five in our nation will experience a nervous disorder serious enough to require medication, hospitalization, and in many cases confinement to an institution.

SYMPTOMS

There are several symptoms which indicate a nervous problem existing or developing. Some of them are: despondency, continual fatigue for no physical reason, undue shyness, headaches, depression, unable to sleep or eat, undue apprehensiveness, irrational fears, fixed ideas, obsessions, destructive attitudes toward self and perhaps toward others.

CAUSES

There is no one cause of nervous disorders. The following does list many contributing factors.

"The mad rush for wealth, the restless desire for change, the pace which is too sharp for many of us, and killing for thousands of us; the noisy, vibrant age in which we live, the widespread use of stimulants and narcotics in alarming amounts, and the lack of self control through over-work, over-strain, and over indulgence — all these serve to roll up an awful array of nervous disorders. These disorders in turn, react upon the central nervous system and exhaust the nerve vitality."

INNER STRENGTH

Does the Spiritual Healing Ministry have a message for the emotionally disturbed? Indeed it does! It brings to you the message of hope and the Person who helps.

The Lord will help you prevent a nervous collapse or to be healed from one. The secret is the inner strength He gives to you.

Many in our age, spiritually speaking, are like a tin can from which all the air has been pumped. It collapses from the normal pressure of the atmosphere. So many people are simply collapsing from the pressures of society because there is nothing within to sustain them. Remember, *"For God hath not given us the spirit of fear, but of power, love, and of a sound mind."* (I Tim. 1:7) Try the following suggestions to overcome your nervous disorder.

I. CONFESSION

Don't try to go it alone. Seek some trusted friend and discuss your fears, real or imagined, which are practically paralyzing you. Also, discuss any guilt which may be upon your heart. This will remove the negative and make room for the positive. It will make more real your confession to God.

II. BELIEVE

Believe what? Believe that you are a child of God! Do not rely upon your feelings, but rely entirely upon His promises. Consider, *"...whosoever calleth upon the Name of the Lord shall be saved."* (Rom. 10:13)

Believe the Lord is with you this very moment. Don't expend time or energy wondering if He will be with you a month, year, or decade from now. He is with you now! (Ps. 23:1)

III. VISUALIZE

Seek to picture yourself as whole. Picture the wholeness you will have instead of the affliction you now have. This is not an escape from reality, but a journey to reality. You must get the eyes of your inner self off of your problems and on the Problem Solver — Jesus.

IV. THANKFULNESS

Begin now to develop the spirit of thankfulness toward God and people. Verbally express thanks to members of your family, to your friends, co-workers, etc. Above all give thanks to God for His many blessings.

V. RELAX

The spirit of quietness is essential. A few minutes a day for you to permit your body and mind to slow down will do wonders. Claim His calmness. *"Be still and know that I am God."* (Ps. 46:10) Talk with the Lord and give Him your problems. He'll take them.

Faith and Healing

I am often asked, *"Is faith a prerequisite to my being healed?"*

I am sure this question is prompted by the many scripture references such as:

"Jesus said unto him, If thou canst believe, all things are possible to him that believeth." (Mark 9:23)

"Therefore I say unto you, What things soever ye desire, when ye pray, believe that ye receive them, and ye shall have them." (Mark 11:24)

"And the Lord said, If ye had faith as a grain of mustard seed, ye might say unto this sycamine tree, Be thou plucked up by the root, and be thou planted in the sea; and it should obey you." (Luke 17:6)

FAITH — A VITAL PART

It is important to realize that faith is a vital part of the healing process. It is important that you believe the Lord wants you to be whole.

It is even of greater importance for you to believe He is able to make you whole.

ACTS OF FAITH

The Lord Jesus commended acts of faith. It was to the woman who touched the hem of His garment that He said, *"...thy faith hath made thee whole..."* (Mt. 9:22)

In like manner He spoke to the centurion, *"...as thou has believed, so be it done unto thee..."* (Mt. 8:13) See also Mark 1:41; 2:5; 10:52.

In addition to these examples of faith and healing Jesus encourages His followers to believe God for great things. In addition to the three verses I list at the beginning of this adventure, please consider: *"...He that believeth on me, the works that I do shall he do also; and greater works than these shall he do; because I go unto my Father."* This reference to John 14:12 certainly applies to Believers today.

It is obvious that faith is an important aspect of healing for you and others.

CORPORATE FAITH

Even though faith is an essential part of our relationship to the Lord, there are many who are healed who do not have great faith. In fact, there are many healed who never expected to be healed.

Why is this? What answers are there for those who question the saint's continued illness and the unbelievers healing?

I feel it is important for us to appreciate corporate faith. It is not simply an individual's faith, but the faith of many people which accounts for many healings.

It is at healing services where the fruit of faith is often seen in the lives of those who seem to have little faith. However, they are in the presence of many with great faith. This corporate faith accomplishes fantastic results.

The Lord is not bound by our human frailties, pet theories, or limited insight into His ways. He is the One whose ways are above our ways. (See Isaiah 55:8-11)

SCRIPTURE REFERENCE

There are several examples of individuals being healed who gave no indication of great faith on their part. Those who brought them to Jesus believed, but the healed one apparently did not. In fact, some of the healed ones were dead and so could not have believed on their own. See:

The withered hand - Mt. 12:9-14
Gergesene demoniacs - Mt. 8:28-34
Slave of the high priest - Luke 22:47-51
Woman infirm for 18 years - Luke 13:10-13
Invalid by the pool - John 5:2-9
Cripple by the Gate Beautiful - Acts 3:1-10
Girl with the spirit of divination - Acts 16:16-18
Father of Publius - Acts 28:7,8
Raising from the dead of:
  Widow's son - Luke 7:11-17
  Lazarus - John 11:38-44
  Dorcas - Acts 9:36-41
  Eutychus - Acts 20:9-12

I feel it is essential that we believe the Lord heals as He wills. We are called to praise and glorify Him forever.

Spiritual Healing and Evangelism

It was in 1973 that over 150 denominations and religious organizations cooperated in a great evangelistic thrust.

The theme for this challenge was *"Calling Our Continent to Christ."* This calling cannot be confined to one year. You and I are constantly called to proclaim the Good News.

THE GIFT OF HEALING

The healing ministry goes hand in hand with a strong emphasis upon evangelism. Healing was very much a part of the commission given to the twelve disciples and to the seventy disciples sent forth by our Lord.

I firmly believe that the gift of healing has been entrusted to His Church to help impart the Good News.

The unbeliever will be converted and the believer strengthened as they witness healings of the body, soul, and spirit.

I appreciate what Emily Gardner Neal says on page 14 of her book, *"The Lord Is Our Healer."*

> *"The healing ministry has opened the way for a return to our once power-filled heritage. Through this ministry God has placed in our hands the one weapon against which the anti-christ cannot survive. He has given us the greatest instrument of conversion the world has known since the time of our Lord."*

THE POWER OF GOD

Our Gospel is more than the proclamation of facts. It is the *"...power of God unto salvation."* (Rom. 1:16) This power was the secret of the early church. They did not keep this secret to themselves, but shared with the whole world the wonderful power of Jesus Christ. Two aspects of healing and evangelism are to be noted.

1. The Lord's healing ministry proclaimed the Good News. This ministry proclaimed the Good News:

A. To the multitudes — *"And all the city was gathered together at the door."* (Mk. 1:33; Mt. 12:15-21; 19:1,2; 14:34-36)

B. To the individual — *"...we know thou art a teacher come from God; for no man can do these miracles that thou doest, except God be with him."* (John 3:2) This chapter will be used by many to stress the need of the New Birth. Most teachers and pastors miss the point that Nicodemus was attracted to Christ because of the Lord's healing ministry.

Nicodemus was not drawn to Christ because of His preaching or teaching skills. It was not because of His devout life or organizational ability. Nicodemus came to Jesus by night because of the healings Jesus did by day.

The Lord's miracles were His evangelistic arm. You and I are called to believe He still is able to reveal Himself through healings.

2. The early church proclaimed the Good News through healings. *"And fear came upon every soul: and wonders and signs were done by the apostles."* (Acts 2:43) *"And the people with one accord gave heed unto those things which Phillip spake, hearing and seeing the miracles which he did." (Acts 8:6)* See also Acts 3:11; Rom. 15:18.19; Heb. 2:4; II Cor. 12:12.

The Spiritual Healing Ministry can be one of the most evangelistic aspects of any congregation. It is a channel the Lord uses.

Overcoming the Fear of Ill Health

Fear is the curse of the world. Especially the fear of ill health.

You should fight this fear as you would the black plague. It should be turned out of your life. It can only entangle you in a web of afflictions and despair.

One who had overcome a disease ridden life gave the following advice. *"Tell those people who are always sick that unresolved problems of fear, hate, jealousy, insecurity and other upsetting emotions can cause physical illness. I know because they kept me a semi-invalid for years."*

I want to present some general characteristics of exaggerated fear of illness.

I. WILD IMAGINATION

Wild imagination is the art of looking for one dreadful disease and then another. The running from physician to physician. The mind becomes geared to a morbid fear of ill health.

II. HYPOCHONDRIA

Hypochondria is the style of life which accents illness. It gives birth to the ingrained habit of being illness centered. Much of your conversation and most of your thoughts deal with illness.

Relentlessly you pursue the *"fads"* for cures and speak disparagingly of physicians and counselors who even hint that your illness may be emotional.

III. SELF-CODDLING

Abnormal fear of ill health will often lead to self-coddling and overprotection of one's well-being. This may lead to your refusal to properly exercise. Further, it helps cover up your laziness and failure to assume rightful responsibility at home or at work.

IV. INTEMPERANCE

The fear of ill health with its many manifestations provides for many the perfect excuse for over-indulgence. It may be in alcohol, drugs, etc.

SOLUTION

If any of the above are part of your life, may I suggest the following.

1. Know who you are fighting. It is the evil one. Illness is not of the Lord. (Acts 10:38)

2. Believe the Lord wants healing and wholeness for you. Really believe this. Do not simply verbalize this thought. (John 10:10)

3. Learn to pray. *"...men ought always to pray and not to faint."* (Luke 18:1) Every person has within the seed of the fear of ill health. Destroy this seed through prayer.

Do not fertilize the seed with fear, discouragement, or negativism. Learn to commune with the Source of Healing, Jesus Christ. May you courageously face your tomorrows with Him.

Remember — *"Courage is fear which has said its prayers."*

4. Discipline your mind to think health. Rebuke thoughts of ill health.

The body is equipped for wholeness. All the resources at its command rush to its defense when it is attacked by disease. There is overwhelming evidence that disease may originate with negative thinking. A change of thinking is more important than a change of pace or climate.

Overcoming the Fear of Death

Christians often say or sing the words, *"Because He lives, I too, I too shall live."*

Yet many Christians possess a morbid fear of death. They are almost paralyzed with the fear of dying. This fear is often manifest in one of the following ways.

I. DWELLING ON DEATH

There is developed the mental habit of dwelling upon the thoughts of death. Even minor illness is perceived as a major issue.

II. LETHARGY

Unbridled thoughts about death will affect every area of your life. You will become a problem to yourself and to others. You may enter a state of despondency and/or depression.

Friends may credit this to outward circumstances when in reality it is because you are plagued with a fear of death.

III. UNREASONABLE ATTITUDE

Many individuals who have a great fear of death develop an unreasonable attitude toward the ordinary risks of life.

They may refuse to ride in an automobile, plane, or train. They may become very suspicious of food prepared by others or purchased from the stores. Also, they may become suspicious of even the natural and harmless actions of others.

IV. UNBELIEVING SPIRIT

Fear is the result of an unbelieving spirit. It is your failure to appropriate the power of His promises.

The fear of death results from the unwillingness to believe that Jesus Christ can deliver the Eternal Life He promised.

CONQUERING THE FEAR OF DEATH

There are several steps which I feel will help you conquer the fear of death. They may appear simple, but they are powerful.

1. Sincerely believe that Christ wants you to enjoy life. The life more abundant is yours for the believing. (John 10:10)

2. Really believe you are born and *re-born* for eternity. God is not dead, nor does He sleep. Jesus not only spoke of the reality of eternal life, but He demonstrated it. The tomb is empty. (Mk. 16:9; Mt. 28:9; 28:16; I Cor. 15:6,7; Lu. 24:15-31; John 20:19,24; John 20:26-28; 21:1-24; Acts 1:2-9)

3. Face the reality that life in this world will end for you. Every person is a terminal case. Longfellow wrote, *"The young may die, but the old must."* The Bible states, *"It is appointed unto man once to die..."* (Heb. 9:27)

The Christian's death should be seen as the act which elevates. It is not a transition which annihilates. It is to be faced by faith and not feared.

4. Develop a life style of service to others. You are called to be a worker *with* God. (I Cor. 3:9)

The mind busy with the concerns of others does not have time to dwell upon death. It is too busy living.

The constant thought of death has misery as its companion. Thoughts centered upon a meaningful life in Christ always have joy as a companion.

5. Realize that occasional thoughts of death are natural. Christians should seek to learn to die well as much as to live well.

It is the constant dwelling upon death which is so devastating to you and yours. Dispense with the fear of death. Live unto Christ.

Overcoming the Fear of Criticism

The critical spirit can be crippling. Many a child, employee, loved one, friend, etc. has been hurt and harmed by undue and often unwise negative criticism.

DEFINITION

The dictionary defines *critical* as:

1. Inclined to find fault or judge with severity.
2. Occupied with or skilled in criticism.

NEGATIVE CRITICISM

The critical spirit seeks to deprive others of their rightful possessions or personality uniqueness.

Thus, the thief criticizes those from whom he steals, the politician speaks disparagingly of the opponent, the neighbor puts down the family next door. Each seeks to be exalted through cutting down others.

It is because of these realities of life that many people develop an unhealthy fear of criticism. You need to realize the seriousness of this fear and to consider its unhealthy consequences.

SELF-CONSCIOUSNESS

A fear of criticism will lead you to become very self-conscious. You will discover it difficult to meet strangers, launch new projects, remain poised in strange situations, or even to maintain a good body posture.

UNSTABLE

The fear of criticism is often what leads to a lack of firmness in making decisions. It will leave you hesitant to develop definite convictions. You will be more inclined to side-step and almost always agree with others without careful examination of their positions. You become a double-minded person and thus unstable in many areas of your life. (James 1:8)

LACK INITIATIVE

The fear of criticism will stifle your initiative. Even wonderful opportunities will not be embraced because you fear what others may say if you fail, or even if you succeed. A fear of criticism is often the reason for a general lack of ambition, mental and physical laziness, undue suspicion of the motives of others, always having an *"excuse"* for your shortcomings, and accepting defeat or quitting.

OVERCOMING

The Good News is that you can overcome the fear of criticism. Consider:

1. Do not expect that all people will always speak well of you. Some individuals have become so negative that they have honed it to a fine art. Jesus warned against wanting all to speak well of you. (Luke 6:26)

2. Remember, many often found fault with Jesus Christ. (Mt. 9:11; 12:2; 15:2; Mk. 2:7; 7:2; Luke 15:2; 19:7; John 6:41)

3. You are to fear God and not man. (Mt. 10:16-39)

4. Develop a meaningful life of private and corporate prayer. Jesus said, *"...ought always to pray and not to faint." (Luke 18:1) He often spent time in prayer. (Mt. 26:41; Mark 1:35; 6:46; Luke 5:15; 6:12; 9:18; 22:41; Eph. 6:18; I Thess. 5:17; I Chr. 16:11)*

5. *Really believe that the Lord is your judge and not people. Prayerfully consider Matthew 10:16-42.*

6. *Keep your eyes on your successes instead of your failures. Thank God for the individuals who encourage you. Seek to die to self, and to live for God and others. You can be unshackled from the fear of criticism. You can be free in the Lord. (II Cor. 3:17)*

Relinquishment

Relinquishment is one of the keys to the victorious Christian life. It is essential to the victory that you desire now and in the future.

SURRENDER

Relinquishment is defined as *"renouncing or surrendering a possession or right,"* or *"to let go."*

In the spiritual sense it is getting rid of self-will. It is the deep conviction that God's will and wisdom is best.

NOT RESIGNATION

Relinquishment is not resignation to blind fate. It is a commitment to a living faith. It is an awareness that God cannot be manipulated or His will bent to yours. However, at the same time it is realizing that God is the Creator and sustainer of all life. He is the Giver of every good and perfect gift. (James 1:17)

There are too many people who want others to be surrendered to the Lord, but are unwilling to make their own surrender. They are like the person who said,

> *"Take my WIFE, and let her be;*
> *Consecrated Lord, to Thee."*

The victory does not come in having your wife or someone else surrender. It is your own life you must surrender unto Him.

RELINQUISHMENT

There are some positive and tangible steps which I suggest will help you relinquish all things unto the Lord.

1. The first point to keep in mind is that relinquishment is commitment to a Person. It is not to a belief or a program. It is to Jesus Christ.

You cannot lean on people. They are not divine, all wise, or all powerful. People will ultimately let you down.

It was because His presence was with him that the Apostle Paul could say, *"...I have learned, in whatsoever state I am, therewith to be content."* (Phil 4:11)

2. Relinquishment comes when you commit to the concept that there is a purpose to your life.

You accept in your heart that in the midst of all the mysteries of life God has a purpose and plan for you. His purposes and plans may be entirely different from your present aims or goals. However, you must accept the fact that He knows what is the very best for you. The Lord Jesus imparted this truth when He said, *"If ye then, being evil, know how to give good gifts to your children, how much more shall your Father which is in heaven give good things to them that ask Him?"* (Mt. 7:11)

Glen Clark wrote, *"God's plan for me is a perfect part of a larger plan. It is designed for the good of all and not for me alone. It is a many-sided Plan and reaches out through all the people I meet. All the events and people who come into my life are instruments for the unfolding of this Plan."*

3. Relinquishment releases spiritual power in and through you. You come to really know that it is *"Not by might nor by power, but by my Spirit says the Lord of Hosts."* (Zechariah 4:6)

The struggling self saps spiritual power. You will drown in your own self-pity and selfishness. Seek to rely on the Lord's promises. He is your answer to your problems.

Many hours after his boat had capsized, a young man was rescued. Why? He had not panicked, but floated the bulk of the time. He let the water support him. Otherwise within a few frantic minutes he would have exhausted his strength and drowned. Relinquishment frees us from foundering in self's waterhole. You can float on God's power and promises. *"...not my will, but thine be done."* (Luke 22:42)

Victory Over Circumstances

Is perfect physical health necessary for a victorious spiritual life? Many would have you belive this is true.

VICTORY

I am fully persuaded that it is wonderful to have a healthy body. However, the victory is not in the physical. The real victory lies much deeper.

"If I had good health..." is the *"If Land"* of many people.

This *"if"* is often used as an excuse for the neglect of the Spiritual Laws. Also, this is used as an excuse for failure to fully develop that person's God given potential.

PHYSICAL MALADY

A physical malady is really no excuse for one's commitment unto the Lord being incomplete.

The truths of Spiritual Healing help us to face ourselves. They help us to triumph in the face of adversity. They help us to achieve victory in the face of adverse circumstances.

Great achievements have often been the fruit of individuals who were physically handicapped. They didn't have perfect physical health, but they had great spirit. They may not have always felt well, but they felt called to great things.

Someone has aptly stated, *"Ninety percent of the work in this world is done by people who don't feel well."*

Consider what some have done even though burdened with physical affliction.

MICHAELANGELO

He was deathly sick off and on throughout his entire life. Severe money problems often plagued him due to the abandonment by his sponsors. Yet, he created monumental works of art and engineering.

TCHAIKOVSKY

His beautiful and moving music gives no hint of the multitude of his problems. He was hopelessly neurotic, fearful of people, terrified of thunderstorms. He even had a fear that sometime his head would fall off while he was conducting.

ELIZABETH BARRETT BROWNING

This most capable poet was an invalid.

BEETHOVEN

He never heard his works played. He heard the sounds in his mind and put them on paper. Beethoven was stone deaf. Yet, he even wrote *Missa Solemnis* which many feel is the most beautiful mass ever written.

COLE PORTER

Most of his songs are known for their bright, cheery, lifting style. However, most of his adult life he suffered from osteomyelitis.

GEORGE GERSHWIN

He wrote popular and classical music until his death. Yet, he suffered from a brain tumor.

PATRICIA NEAL

She suffered three near fatal strokes and had to learn to walk and talk again. Further, her young son became hydrocephalic resulting from a bus accident. One of her daughters died. In spite of these tragedies she sprang back to be honored for her acting skills.

RICHARD WAGNER

His beautiful music gave no hint of his being deaf.

THE SPECIAL TRAIT

One of the special traits each of the above possessed was the ability to forget the *"ifs."* They may have stumbled, but they never stayed down. See Phil. 4:19.

Action or Alibis

Each of us is called to "act" upon the promises of God. There are hundreds of promises in His Holy Word. Our response toward these promises should be like Paul's.

> " *And being fully persuaded that, what he had promised, he was able also to perform."* (Rom. 4:21)

This verse sets the pace for the way we should act upon His precious promises. Life is not to defeat, but to make us. Trusting in His promises is a big step toward our victory.

SOME PROMISES

The following are just a few of the promises, which have been given to all believers.

> *"And we know that all things work together for good to them that love God, to them who are the called according to his purpose."* (Rom. 8:28)
>
> *"Jesus said unto him, if thou canst believe, all things are possible to him that believeth."* (Mk. 9:23)
>
> *"Therefore I say unto you, What things soever ye desire, when ye pray, believe that ye receive them, and ye shall have them."* (Mk. 11:24)

IF LAND

There are far too many unwilling to really believe God's promises.

They choose to wallow in the stagnant pool of *"If Land."* They are thoroughly convinced if things were different now, or if they had been different, life would be great.

How foolish to let your life be determined by the *"ifs."* Which of the following *"ifs"* do you use as an excuse?

If I had a good education.....
If I had enough *"pull"*.....
If I didn't have a wife and family.....
If I only had a wife and children.....
If I had money.....
If I could get the right job.....
If I had good health.....
If I only had time.....
If times were better.....
If other people really understood me.....
If conditions around me were different.....
If I could live my life over again.....
If I did not fear what *"they"* will say.....
If I had been given a fair chance.....
If I just got a break.....
If other people didn't have it in for me.....
If I were only younger.....
If nothing happens to stop me.....
If I could only do what I want.....
If I had been born rich.....
If I could meet *"the right"* people.....
If I had the talent some people have.....
If I dared to assert myself.....
If I didn't have to keep house and look after the children.....
If I only had somebody to help me.....
If I lived in a big city.....
If I were only free.....
If I could get away to the country.....
If I had the personality of some people.....
If I were not so fat.....
If I could just get a break.....
If the boss only appreciated me.....
If my family would get off my back.....
If I could only get out of debt.....
If everybody didn't oppose me.....
If I had married the *"right"* person.....
If people weren't so dumb.....
If luck were not against me.....
If I lived in a different neighborhood.....
If I had a different pastor.....
If the people in the church were really spiritual.....
If other people would only listen to me.....
If I didn't have to work so hard.....
If my wife really understood me.....
If my husband would really listen to me.....
If God would really show Himself to me.....

The list of *"ifs"* is endless. I would encourage you to depart from *"If Land"* and dwell in the land of God's certainties.

May you view every alibi as a temptation of Satan. Resist it and live victoriously.

Why an Eye Surgeon Believes in Spiritual Healing

Dr. Clair B. King served many years as an eye surgeon and highly respected physician. He is a very close personal friend of mine and I asked his permission to publish why he believes in Spiritual Healing.

The following are some of the reasons he gave for his becoming an enthusiastic ambassador for the message of Spiritual Healing.

A SPIRITUAL BEING

"Man is made up of body, soul, and spirit. The three are intricately interwoven. It is wrong to think that when man is physically ill he should seek only medical help. All illnesses have their spiritual component.

SKEPTICAL AT FIRST

"I must admit that at first I was very skeptical of Spiritual Healing. I feel most doctors feel as I felt. However, the more I studied about it the more I was convinced.

"The study of the Bible and other books concerning healing helped me to accept its message. I arrived at the conclusion that Spiritual Healing has a major role to play in the healing process.

MORE THAN PSYCHOSOMATIC

"Physicians are discovering there may be a lack of complete healing until the soul is also considered in the search for health. Psychosomatic medicine recognizes the power of disorders of the mind such as anxiety, stress, strain, etc.

"These may cause diseases of the body such as ulcers, high blood pressure, heart diseases and many other afflictions. However, the wholeness Christ imparts to the body, mind, and soul is not the same as psychosomatic medicine.

WEAKNESS OF MEDICINE

"The physician is not trained to treat spiritual ills such as hate, jealousy, pride, envy, resentment, and guilt. Yet, these spiritual ills have a dominating influence over both soul and body.

"Christ is the answer in the cure of them.

THE GREAT PHYSICIAN

"I believe the ministries of the Church are wonderful channels of God's healing. They enable the power of the Living Christ to bring healing.

"The ill should receive the ministries of the Church, not as a last resort, but concurrently with medical treatment.

SALVATION IS WHOLENESS

"Jesus came to bring us salvation. This includes wholeness of body, soul, and spirit.

"God is on the side of good health in all three of these areas. He is actively working toward your good health and mine. Jesus said, *'Ask, and it shall be given you; seek, and ye shall find; knock, and it shall be opened unto you.'* (Mt. 7:7)

"God does not force good health on anyone any more than He forces us to be sinless.

ALL HEALING OF GOD

"All healing is of God. He uses the physician, the surgeon, the psychiatrist, the nurse, pharmacist, technician, etc.

"However, He alone is the Source of healing. He can also cure disease without help from any of us. After all, He made us and not we ourselves.

"Our little finite minds will never understand His infinite power. In fact, with Him there are no incurable diseases or unsolvable problems. There are too many cases of healings through prayer to simply explain such happenings as coincidence or mis-diagnosis. The Lord is in the healing business."

Do Physical Healings Still Occur?

The earthly ministry of our Lord included many physical healings. Consider one occasion where He used them as proof of His Messiahship. (Mt. 11:4-5)

Physical healings were not confined to our Lord. He instructed His disciples to heal. *"And as ye go, preach saying; The Kingdom of heaven is at hand. Heal the sick, cleanse the lepers, raise the dead, cast out devils."* (Mt. 10:7-8)

After the resurrection the disciples were the instruments for many healings. The book of Acts records nine individual physical healings and on seven occasions speaks of multiple healings.

Paul, in his epistles, often speaks of signs and wonders and of the gift of healing. (I Cor. 12:9; II Cor. 12:12; Rom. 15:18-19)

A question I am often asked is, *"But do physical healings still occur today?"* I can truthfully answer, *"Indeed they do!"* The power of the Lord has not been withdrawn. The arm of God is not shortened.

Below are a few of the physical healings I have witnessed.

ARTHRITIS

An individual attended our healing service. She had severe arthritis in her hands. They were swollen, her fingers drawn, and pain was always present. The Lord gave a healing and the pain was gone as well as the swelling and stiffness.

WHIPLASH

Another case is the woman in terrible pain and discomfort because of an auto accident. A neck injury was getting progressively worse. Even her walk was being reduced to a shuffle. Reluctantly she consented to the pleas of her friends to come to me for Laying-on-of-Hands.

The moment I offered the brief prayer she felt something happen to her. The pain was gone and she could walk normally. She was a different person physically, emotionally and spiritually. She was changed from a discouraged, disgruntled, and defeated Christian to a victorious and witnessing dynamo for Christ.

RIGHT HAND

May I give another accident victim as a witness of the power of the Lord to heal today.

This lady had recovered beautifully from many injuries. However, her right hand continued to be practically useless years after the accident.

Long and arduous physical therapy had restored partial usage in the hand. She attended a healing service at our church.

You can imagine how thrilled she was to awaken the next morning to discover that her afflicted hand was normal.

SKIN DISEASE

The most spectacular physical healing I have witnessed was a friend of mine in his seventies. He was bedfast with a rare skin disease. His entire body was covered with an itching, seeping, painful rash. He endured constant pain. His wife had to change his shorts four or five times a day because of the seeping.

One Saturday he requested anointing with oil. Two other men and myself went to his home and anointed him. Early the next morning his wife phoned and asked us to stop by before church. When we arrived he was sitting up in bed pulling off pieces of skin in strips about 4 or 5 inches long and about an inch wide. His bedside wastebasket was already nearly one-fourth full of this diseased skin. He continued throughout the day to peel off all the diseased skin and to his amazement, and ours, discovered perfect skin underneath. He was completely healed and lived to be over ninety years of age.

Space prohibits other examples. Suffice to say though, that Christ does heal today. I feel that my efforts in the healing ministry would have been amply rewarded if only one had been healed. Praise the Lord there have been many healed. It is to Him that I give the glory and honor.

Martin Luther and Healing

Did the Reformers believe in the Lord's healing power? Have the devout men of God through the ages believed in the power of the Lord to heal? Is healing a new fad and one which will fade in the years ahead?

These and many other questions come to the sincere seeker after the truth of healing in the church.

It is reported that Martin Luther wrote the following letter to Pastor Severin Schulze on June 1, 1545.

It certainly reveals Luther's belief in the power of prayer, and also in his belief of the Lord's ability and desire to heal.

I have put in *italics* the references to prayer. I feel this will accent Luther's practice of Christian concern through prayer.

Venerable Sir and Pastor,

The tax collector in Torgau and the councilor in Belgern have written me to ask that I offer some good advice and help for Mr. John Korner, afflicted husband. I know of no worldly help to give. If the physicians are at a loss to find a remedy, you may be sure that it is not a case of ordinary melancholy. It must rather, be an affliction that comes from the devil, and this must be counteracted by the power of Christ and with *prayer of faith*. This is what we do, and that we have been accustomed to do, for a cabinet maker here was similarly afflicted with madness and we cured him by *prayer* in Christ's name.

Accordingly you should proceed as follows: Go to him with a deacon and two or three good men. Confident that you, as Pastor of the place, are clothed with the authority of the ministerial office, lay your hands upon him and say,

"Peace be with you, dear brother, from God our Father and from our Lord Jesus Christ."

Thereupon repeat the Creed and the Lord's Prayer over him in a clear voice, and close with these words:

"O God, Almighty Father, who has told us through Thy Son, verily, verily, I say unto you, whatsoever ye shall ask the Father in my Name, He will give it to you: who has commanded and encouraged us to *pray* in His Name 'Ask and you shall receive;' and who in like manner has said, 'Call upon me in the day of trouble; I will deliver thee, and thou shalt glorify me;' we unworthy sinners, relying on these words and commands *pray* for the mercy with such faith as we can muster.

"Graciously deign to free this man from all evil, and put to nought the work that Satan has done in him, to the honor of thy Name and the strengthening of the faith of believers; through the same Jesus Christ Thy Son, our Lord, who liveth and reigneth with thee, world without end, Amen."

Then, when you depart, lay hands upon the man again and say,

"These signs shall follow them that believe; they shall lay hands on the sick and they shall recover."

Do this three times, once on each of three successive days. Meanwhile let *prayers* be said from the chancel of the church, publicly until God hears them.

Insofar as we are able, we shall at the same time unite our faithful *prayers* and *petitions* to the Lord with yours.

Farewell, other counsel than this I do not have.

I remain,

Martin Luther

John Wesley and Spiritual Healing

Many of the great Christians through the centuries have believed in the Lord's healing power. This was an important part of the ministry of John Wesley.

He firmly believed that the Lord desired to send His healing. He had confidence in the power of the Lord to heal. Consider the following incidents reported by Wesley.

SPOTTED FEVER

"...I visited several of the sick. Most of them were ill of the spotted fever, which, they informed me, had been extremely mortal, few persons recovering from it. But God had said, *'Hitherto shalt thou come.'* I believe that there was not one with whom we were, but recovered."

THE CONFINED

His *JOURNAL* discloses, "...I was desired to visit one who had been eminently pious, but had now been confined to her bed for several months, and was utterly unable to raise herself up. She desired us to pray that the chain might be broken. A few of us prayed in faith. Presently she rose up, dressed herself, came downstairs, and I believe had not any further complaint."

In a letter to Alexander Knox he wrote, "...He wants to give you and my dear Mrs. Knox both inward and outward health. And why not now? Surely all things are ready: believe, and receive the blessing. ...Look up, and wait for happy days."

SORE THROAT

Consider what happened to Wesley when he was 86 years old. He found himself so hoarse he could neither sing nor preach. A large congregation had assembled to hear the gospel message. Wesley reports, "I trusted in God, and began to speak. The more I spoke, the more my voice was strengthened, so that in a few minutes I think all could hear; and many, I believe, took knowledge that what they heard was not the word of man, but of God."

Wesley's confidence in the Lord seemed to constantly abound. One woman was in great pain. After Wesley prayed for her she received such relief that immediately she arose and went about her work. Previously to his becoming a very famous clergyman, Thomas Merrick was healed from a critical illness. He was near to the door of death when Wesley and some other believers prayed for him.

LAYING-ON-HANDS

Wesley firmly believed that distance did not limit the power of prayer. However, at the same time he believed and practiced the ministry of laying-on-hands for the ill. This he considered an apostolic injunction to be followed by the believers of his day.

RIGHT WITH GOD

Insistence upon right relations to the Lord was central to Wesley's ministry. He felt that God's plan was to heal the soul and body together. Thus he insisted upon the individual getting *"right"* with God, and trusting for healing. The Lord has *"good things"* in store for His believers. This conviction made it possible for Wesley to minister to the practical needs of people of his day.

CHRISTIAN PIETY

Wesley tried to get individuals to live a life of deep Christian piety. He knew that violent passions were dangerous to health. The soul which remained calm in the Lord would more likely remain strong in body.

He says, *"And by the unspeakable joy and perfect calm, serenity, and tranquility it gives the mind, it becomes the most powerful of all the means of health and long life."* Wesley saw the love of God as preventive medicine.

The Presbyterian Church and Healing

"The Relation of Christian Faith to Health" is a comprehensive report adopted by the General Assembly of the United Presbyterian Church USA in 1960.

The report was prepared by a committee of prominent Presbyterians, including several physicians. Clergy and laity alike will find encouragement for the Healing Ministry from this report. Some important excerpts follow.

CONQUERING EVIL

"The redemption which God in Jesus Christ brings to the world through His Church is sufficient for the ultimate conquest of every evil. Among the evils from which God in Christ is able to redeem man are the myriad forms of physical and mental illness. It is plainly the understanding of the New Testament that health in body, mind and spirit is the ultimate will of God. The conquest of various diseases and infirmities is one of the chief evidences given in the New Testament for believing that God in Christ is overcoming the power of evil. The Church of Jesus Christ has a ministry to the sick which cannot be compartmentalized or limited.

THE CHURCH & SUFFERING

"Nothing is more indicative of the Church's fidelity to Christ than her care of the sick and the handicapped. The Church has something to offer sufferers which the world cannot give. The Church must reach out to those in need with what she has, namely, with the Gospel of Jesus Christ who came that men might have life *'...and have it more abundant.'* (John 10:10)

COOPERATION NEEDED

"The Church's ministry to the sick is not a substitute for medical care. The callings of Christian nurses, and other members of the physical and mental team are of Christ. The time has come for all vocational groups involved in the healing process to understand and cooperate with one another in a work that includes them all.

CHRIST'S MINISTRY

"The earthly ministry of Jesus Christ set the pattern for the Christian Church and it is to Him that we must look for guidance and instruction in the healing aspect of our ministry today.

"It is important that the Church make a fresh study of biblical teaching regarding the relation of Christian faith and health. Such a study will show that the healing of physical and mental illnesses was indeed a part of our Lord's work and is intended to be a part of His disciples' work in every generation.

PREVENTIVE & CURATIVE

"The Church's ministry to the sick is both preventive and curative. Health is not an end in itself, but a means of serving God. We are interested in health because we want to serve God to the best of our ability.

WHY JESUS HEALED

"Jesus healed out of mercy in the knowledge that it is God's will to deliver men from all kinds of evil, including physical and mental illness.

"He prayed and worked for the removal of suffering. He regarded the healings which took place as so many signs of God's power breaking in upon the kingdom of evil. Healings were regarded as certain signs of God's nearness, portents of the age to come when all mourning and crying and pain would be done away. (Rev. 21:4)

NEW TESTAMENT TEACHES

"During His earthly ministry our Lord sent out His disciples to preach, teach, and heal. ...Christ directed His Church to heal and...gave it power to do so."

The Presbyterian Church and Spiritual Healing
(continued)

"All healing is Divine. God is the author of the natural world and all its creatures, including man. It is by His power that the universe and man are sustained. Natural law is God's law. Some of the mechanisms of healing are understood; but as it has been so often pointed out, the doctor dresses the wound, but the Lord heals. All healing is of God, whether it occurs through what we call natural law or according to laws we do not know. Many laws remain undiscovered.

ILLNESS IS AN EVIL

"Illness is an evil. Jesus Christ regarded illness as something to be overcome. He coped with illness, and he conquered it. It was His teaching that God wills healing. For the Christian, whether physician or layperson, the compassionate and effective ministry of Christ to the sick is an inspiration and a challenge to overcome this evil with good.

BRING YOUR NEEDS

"Within the Christian understanding of Fellowship with God there is room for lifting physical and mental needs to God in prayer. Jesus taught us to do this.

"We must recognize the limits and the possibilities of not only the established therapies, but of new ones such as the discipline of prayer.

"This is a time for exploration and experimentation in the religious dimension of healing. God has many therapies, and it is contrary to the spirit of science as well as to the faith of Christianity to absolutize any therapeutic method.

SPIRITUAL NEEDS

"Great and grave as the dangers in *"faith healing"* are, there is the equally great danger of limiting the power of God to work in the Church because of timidity and fear. Non-medical ministries to the sick have a vital place because the sick have spiritual needs.

TYPES OF MINISTRIES

"We recommend that Pastors consider the possibilities inherent in this report for the extension of their pastoral ministries to the sick by means of public worship, Christian Education, small groups and the possible use of services related to the physical and mental needs of members of the congregation.

HELP BY THE SESSION

"We recommend that Session help the Pastor to develop an adequate program of shepherding the congregation and that they assist the Pastor in initiating and maintaining an effective program in this area.

THE BOOK OF ACTS

"The Book of Acts contains a number of general statements to the effect that the Church continued to heal after the death and resurrection of Christ. For example:

"And more than ever believers were added to the Lord, multitudes both of men and women, so that they even carried out the sick into the streets, and laid them on beds and pallets, that as Peter came by at least his shadow might fall on some of them. The people also gathered from towns around Jerusalem, bringing the sick and those afflicted with unclean spirits, and they were all healed." (Acts 5:14-16)

You may also want to consider: Acts 3:1-10; 9:17-19; 9:36-42; 16:16-18; 28:3-6; 28:7,8.

The above quotations are from: "The Relation of Christian Faith to Health," United Presbyterian Church USA 1960.

The Lord's Provision For Wholeness

Dr. R. A. Torrey in his book, *"Divine Healing,"* says:

"Just as one gets the firstfruits of his spiritual salvation in the life that now is, so we get the firstfruits of our physical salvation in the life that now is...The Gospel of Christ has salvation for the body as well as for the soul...The atoning death of Jesus Christ secured for us not only physical healing, but also the resurrecting and perfecting and glorifying of our bodies."

The beloved John wrote, *"Beloved, I wish above all things that thou mayest prosper and be in health, even as thy soul prospereth."* (III John v.2)

The Lord does desire wholeness for you. He has made ample provision for you to receive and to maintain this wholeness. He can and will meet your physical and spiritual needs.

The Old Testament presents redemptive names for God. Even the meaning of the names reveal the Lord's desire for your wholeness.

JEHOVAH-JIREH

JEHOVAH-JIREH — "The Lord will provide." (Gen. 22:14 RSV) The Lord was capable and willing to provide the offering in that day. He is still providing all that you need.

We know that Christ is the perfect offering for each and every person. He is our fullness and our wholeness.

JEHOVAH-RAPHA

JEHOVAH-RAPHA — "I am the Lord that healeth thee." (Ex. 15:26) The privilege of wholeness is provided for you in Christ's atonement. Even the prophet of old pointedly presents the reality of your wholeness in and through the atonement of Christ. (Isa. 53:4,5)

Matthew believed that the prophet was speaking of what our Lord accomplished. (Mt. 8:17)

The writer of Hebrews clinches it when he says, *"Jesus Christ the same yesterday, and today, and forever."* (Heb. 13:8) Christ had, has now, and always will have the power to heal. He heals you.

JEHOVAH-NISSI

JEHOVAH-NISSI — "The Lord is our Banner." (Ex. 17:15 RSV) The Lord is our leader. He ever sets the pace. You can believe that He heals to the utmost.

Our Banner implies that He goes before you in all matters and situations of life. You are called to believe and to receive from Him. He does go before you in all things and all days.

JEHOVAH-SHALOM

JEHOVAH-SHALOM — "The Lord is Peace." (Judg. 6:23,24 RSV) Your life need not be ruined by restlessness and despair. The Lord has provided for your peace.

The wholeness millions are seeking is peace. This peace is from the Lord. This peace has truly been given through Jesus Christ our Great Physician.

Speaking of peace the prophet said, *"...the chastisement of our peace was upon him..."* (Isa. 53:5) Jesus said, *"...my peace I give unto you..."* (John 14:27) St. Paul said, *"...peace of God...through Christ Jesus..."* (Phil. 4:7)

JEHOVAH-TSIDKENU

JEHOVAH-TSIDKENU — "The Lord Our Righteousness." (Jer. 23:6) Many exist with lives of defeat because of guilt. They fail to realize the Lord has provided wholeness for them in this area.

The promise of the Lord is that His righteousness is imputed and imparted to you. (Gen. 15:6; Acts 13:39; Rom. 5:1)

JEHOVAH-SHAMMA

JEHOVAH-SHAMMA — "The Lord is there." (Ezek. 48:35) There is never a moment of any given day, but what the Lord is there to help. This promise is abundantly fulfilled in Christ's words, *"...I am with you always..."* (Mt. 28:20)

All that is revealed in the Names have been fulfilled in the redemptive act of Christ. He is your all. Believe Him for your wholeness.

The By-Products of Illness

Some years ago my friend, Dr. Clair B. King, M.D., was confined to the hospital. His account of this experience vividly depicts our triune nature.

His story clearly demonstrates the devastating by-products of illness. Illness does not bring positive creativity but destructive attitudes and actions.

ARTHRITIS

"I entered the hospital for treatment of a physical ailment — chronic arthritis of the 7th and 8th cervical vertebrae. This was causing some pressure on the left ulnar nerve resulting in pain in the region of the shoulder blade radiating down the left arm to my elbow and some numbness and weakness of the left arm. I was to be put in traction and since I was feeling otherwise well, I took along plenty of books and other reading material.

HONG KONG FLU

"Two days after entering the hospital I contracted Hong Kong Flu with fever, crushing headache, epigastric pain radiating upward to the region of the heart, gastritis, nausea, vomiting, cough and other aches and pains.

"For a period of three days I couldn't eat anything and neither could I sleep at night. I was very ill — so ill that I didn't care whether *"school"* kept or not. An internist was called in consultation and ordered repeated electrocardiograms, a GI x-ray series and daily blood tests. All of these complicated my traction treatments.

SPIRITUALLY ILL

"When I entered the hospital I had simply a physical disorder, but soon found that I was affected mentally and spiritually as well. I literally found out that I was made up of more than a body.

"As I grew worse I found that I could no longer read or even watch television or listen to radio. And so as I lay awake I tried to recall and repeat certain Psalms I had committed to memory and knew very well. My memory failed me and I couldn't recall certain parts of familiar Psalms. I had trouble figuring out the day and the date.

"Then I began to develop resentments against the nurses whom previously I felt had been so kind. I now resented the bed, the pillow, visitors who stayed too long, even my doctor who didn't come as often as I thought he should nor give orders I thought should be given. I even refused to take some medicine and took medicine which was not prescribed. In other words, I developed into a *"bad"* patient.

PRAYERS

"One thing I was grateful for was the assurance of my friends that they were praying for me. I also appreciated those who came to my bedside to pray for me.

"I had reached the place where my prayers consisted of three words, *"Lord help me!"* I found myself saying these words over and over again. I, deep down in my heart, knew that God answers prayers. As a matter of fact, it was when I was at my lowest ebb that I realized the prayers were being answered and I started to recover.

RECOVERY

"Gradually my headache ceased, my stomach settled down, my tests came back negative, the fever passed, and my mind cleared. I was able to get some sleep. I was able to keep some food down. My resentments passed away, my strength started to return and I was soon able to come home.

"I experienced a new realization that man is indeed a trinity — body, soul, and spirit. I found out that I harbored resentments just the same as everyone. I had a good demonstration that the whole person is ill."

The Seriously Ill and Spiritual Healing

The seriously ill patient is often lonely, discouraged, despondent, too weak or too full of medication to think logically, in pain, resentful toward God and man for his problem or illness.

A PERSONAL WITNESS

The witness of my dear friend, Dr. King, as to what happened to him during his hospital confinement bears repeating. He wrote:

"When I entered the hospital I had simply a physical disorder, but soon I found that I was affected mentally and spiritually as well...As I grew worse, I could no longer read, watch TV, or listen to the radio.

"I tried to recall certain Psalms I had committed to memory, but my memory failed me, and I couldn't recall certain parts of them. I had trouble figuring out the day and date. I began to develop resentments against the nurses who previously I felt were so kind. I resented the bed, the pillow, the visitors who stayed too long, even my doctor who didn't come as often as I thought he should nor give orders I thought he should. I even refused to take some medicine, and took medicine that was not prescribed."

His account conveys the trauma of a seriously ill person. I would like to suggest the following guidelines for ministering unto the seriously ill patient.

ALL CHANNELS

You should remember that the Lord heals through many channels. He uses medicine, physician, (even though some may not acknowledge the source of all healings), prayer, confession, absolution, anointing, belief in His promises, etc. The patient is a spiritual being and must have the spiritual ministry of the church. You cannot simply minister to the body and meet his complete needs.

RASH PROMISES

There should never be any rash promises of physical healing offered to the patient or to members of his family. You cannot guarantee physical healing.

CALLED TO BE FAITHFUL

No one, be he physician or pray-er, can claim credit for recovery. Neither should one assume unnecessary blame if death occurs.

We are called to be faithful in our ministry and not *"successful"* according to some men's standards or expectations.

OPTIMISM

A spirit of optimism should characterize the Spiritual Healing Ministry. *"Where there is life, there is hope."*

There are no hopeless or incurable cases with Jesus Christ. There are innumerable cases of individuals recovering and living for many years when it appeared as if their death during a severe illness was certain.

VISITS

Visits with the seriously ill should be brief and limited to the family, a few close friends, and the pastor.

The pastor and others should minister with prayer and frequent references to God's many precious promises. He is not to be the bearer of despair, but must always bring the good news of Christ even in the darkest hour.

All friends can minister by sending cards, letters, and through their prayers.

ANOINTING

The anointing with oil should be understood as a step to life and not the last rites.

Since it is almost impossible to instruct in moments of extreme illness it is important that Christians be taught from childhood up concerning anointing with oil.

When the need for it arises, patients will receive it in the right spirit if they have been properly instructed previously.

OUR GOAL — JESUS CHRIST

The primary goal of all the efforts of Spiritual Healing is to bring individuals to Christ. He is relevant to our day.

The Importance of Fasting

Fasting and prayer are so closely linked that they both should be a part of the disciplined life of every believer.

In his book, *"God's Chosen Fast,"* Arthur Wallis has well stated:

"Fasting is important, more important, perhaps than many of us have supposed. For all that it is not a major biblical doctrine, a foundation stone of the faith, or a panacea for every spiritual ill. Nevertheless, when exercised with a pure heart and a right motive, fasting may provide us a window opening up new horizons in the unseen world; a spiritual weapon of God's proving..."

It is obvious that fasting was an important part of the life of many of God's leaders through the centuries.

We have many Biblical examples of individuals fasting. Moses, David, Elijah, Daniel, Hannah, Anna, Paul, Barnabas all come to mind. Even our Lord began His public ministry with 40 day of prayer and fasting.

CHRIST'S TEACHING

Our Lord did not eliminate fasting from the disciplined spiritual life.

He took for granted that any sincere believer would be fasting from time to time. He did not present fasting as an option. He taught that our pilgrimage of faith includes times of fasting. He did not say, *"If you fast,"* but he confidently said, *"When you fast..."*

"Moreover when you fast, be not, as the hypocrites, of a sad countenance: ...but thou, when thou fastest, anoint thine head and wash thy face." (Mt. 6:16-18)

Jesus approached fasting as He did prayer and contributing to the needy. He simply took for granted that believers would fast.

He took this as much for granted as He did that believers would pray and that they would share what they have with others.

There were no *"ifs"* or *"buts"* about the spiritual discipline of fasting. Fasting and praying were a part of our Lord's disciplined life and He wanted them to be a part of the disciplined life of His followers.

"And when thou prayest..." (Mt. 6:5-7)
"...when thou doest alms..." (Mt. 6:1-4)
"...when ye fast..." (Mt. 6:16)

FOCUSED ON THE LORD

One of the practical aspects of fasting is that it helps you to get your mind off of yourself and unto others and the Lord.

Many in our nation have so much they have become spiritually flabby. Overeating and improper eating habits can lead to many problems in our physical body.

Lack of discipline in the midst of abundance in the things of the spirit can lead to spiritual heart trouble. Ultimately spiritual heart trouble is more devastating to you than is physical heart trouble.

Moses realized the spiritual dangers of abundance. He said, *"...lest when thou hast eaten and art full, hast goodly houses...herds and flocks multiply, thy silver and gold is multiplied,...then thine heart be lifted up, and thou forget the Lord thy God..."* (Deut. 8:11-14)

The prophet Hosea graphically reveals that the fears of Moses were not unfounded. He says, *"...they were filled, and their heart was exalted; therefore they have forsaken me."* (Hosea 13:6)

Misuse and abuse of abundance were sins of Sodom. We usually think only of their sin of homosexuality. Notice carefully the indictment of the prophet Ezekiel. He does not minimize the horrible sin of Sodomy, but he puts his finger on a very real problem which is often neglected. *"Your sister Sodom's sins were pride and laziness and too much food, while the poor and needy suffered outside her door."* (Ez. 16:49 LB)

Fasting is doing by choice what many must do of necessity. It is abstaining from food. It goes further and permits the spiritual to be accented. It is a conscious effort to cease to always serve the flesh. It is for our day.

The Bible and Fasting

Fasting was definitely a part of the life of many of the individuals of Biblical times. It has been a spiritual practice on the part of the devout through the centuries.

The Church of our day needs to stress the positive privileges and power of fasting. It is my prayer the Christians today will seek the Lord's forgiveness as never before.

TYPES OF FASTING

There are three basic types of fasting mentioned in Scripture. All are for a limited period of time and observed on many different occasions and many different reasons. They are as follows:

1. The Normal Fast — This is the abstaining from all forms of food, but not from water.

2. The Absolute Fast — This involves the abstaining from all food and all liquids.

3. The Partial Fast — This is curtailing, but not completely eliminating one's intake of food and drink.

I have listed below the references to fasting in the Old and New Testaments.

OLD TESTAMENT REFERENCES TO FASTING

1.	Exod. 34:28	By Moses
2.	Lev. 23:14	Until the wave offering
3.	Num. 6:3,4	The Nazarite Law
4.	Deut. 9:9,18	By Moses
5.	Judges 20:26	by Israel
6.	I Sam. 1:7,8	By Hannah
7.	I Sam. 7:6	At Mizpah
8.	I Sam. 14:24-30	Saul's battle instructions
9.	I Sam. 20:34	Jonathan grieved
10.	I Sam. 28:20	Saul before his death
11.	I Sam. 31:13 & I Chron. 10:12	By those who buried Saul
12.	II Sam. 1:12	David and his men
13.	II Sam. 3:35	David at Abner's death
14.	II Sam. 12:16-23	David at son's death
15.	I Kings 13:8-25	By Prophet
16.	I Kings 19:4-8	By Elijah
17.	I Kings 21:9,12	When Naboth set on high
18.	I Kings 21:27	By Ahab
19.	II Chron. 20:3	Proclaimed by Jehoshaphat
20.	Ezra 8:21-23	Proclaimed by Ezra
21.	Ezra 10:6	By Ezra
22.	Neh. 1:4	By Nehemiah
23.	Neh. 9:1	By people of Jerusalem
24.	Esther 4:3	By the Jews
25.	Esther 4:16	Called by Esther
26.	Esther 9:31	Feast of Purim
27.	Psalm 35:13	Psalmist for the sick
28.	Psalm 69:10	The soul chastened
29.	Psalm 109:24	The cause of weakness
30.	Isa. 58:1-14	Fasting which pleases God
31.	Jer. 14:10-12	Fasting which displeases God
32.	Jer. 36:5-10	A Day of Fasting
33.	Dan. 1:12-16	Limited Food Consumption
34.	Dan. 6:18	By Darius
35.	Dan. 9:3	By Daniel
36.	Dan. 10:2,3	Daniel's partial fast
37.	Joel 1:14	Sanctify a Fast
38.	Joel 2:12	When returning to God
39.	Joel 2:15	Sanctify a Fast
40.	Jonah 3:5-9	By people of Nineveh
41.	Zech. 7:3-5	Fifth & Seventh months
42.	Zech. 8:19	4th; 5th; 7th; 9th months

NEW TESTAMENT REFERENCES TO FASTING

1.	Mt. 4:2; Lu. 4:2	By our Lord
2.	Mt. 6:16-18	Not as hypocrites
3.	Mt. 9:14; Mk. 2:18; Lu. 5:33	John's disciples & Pharisees
4.	Mt. 9:15; Mk. 2:19; Lu. 5:34	When bridegoom departed
5.	Mt. 11:18; Lu. 7:33	John the Baptist
6.	Mt. 15:32; Mk. 8:3	The four thousand
7.	(Mt. 17:21); (Mk. 9:29)	Prayer and fasting
8.	Lu. 2:37	By Anna
9.	Lu. 18:12	By boastful Pharisee
10.	Acts 9:9	By Saul of Tarsus
11.	(Acts 10:30)	By Cornelius
12.	Acts. 13:2,3	At Antioch
13.	Acts 14:23	Appointment of Elders
14.	Acts 23:12-21	Jews desiring to kill Paul
15.	Acts 27:9	Day of Atonement
	See: Lev. 16:29; 23:27,32; Num. 29:7	
16.	Acts 27:21,33	By those with Paul
17.	(I Cor. 7:5)	In Marriage relationship
18.	II Cor. 6:5	Part of a faithful ministry
19.	II Cor. 11:27	Among Paul's sufferings

In ( ) are references to fasting in the King James Version, which are omitted by most later versions.

Spiritual Healing and Fasting

Spiritual wholeness is a demanding life. In fact, physical, spiritual, and emotional wholeness demands dedicated devotion to God's laws.

One of the avenues to vitality of body, soul, and spirit is fasting. Sad, but true, this discipline of the Christian life is often completely neglected by most believers.

I am one who believes that the ministry of Spiritual Healing cannot be pursued to the fullest if fasting is neglected. It must be included. Saints through the ages have told us that fasting helps cultivate the presence and power of the Lord.

WHAT IS FASTING?

The dictionary definition of fasting is abstinence from food, partial or total, or from prescribed kinds of foods, for a limited period of time.

The word, *faest*, meaning *firm* or *fixed*, is the Anglo-Saxon word from which our word, *fast*, is derived. Thus fast simply means to fasten or hold one's self from food.

THE BIBLE AND FASTING

There are dozens of references to fasting in the Bible. I call your attention to the following occasions of fasting as revealed in the scriptures.

a. Fasting in times of national crises. (II Chr. 21:3; Esther 4:16)

b. To escape God's judgment. (Jonah 3:5)

c. As a sign of repentance. (I Sam. 7:6)

d. When in close fellowship with God. (Ex. 34:28) - Moses

e. In the face of personal dangers and difficulties. (I Kings 19:20) - Elijah

f. When burdened for others. (Ezra 10:6)

g. For spiritual insight. (Daniel 10:3)

h. As Church leaders are chosen and commissioned. (Acts 13:2; 14:23)

i. As a practice endorsed by the Lord Jesus (Luke 4:1,2)

Some Christians infer that Jesus discouraged fasting. They teach he did away with all ritual.

A careful study of the Scriptures will reveal otherwise. He practiced fasting. This was especially true during the 40 days of His temptation.

He gave a strong and positive endorsement of fasting. *"But thou, when thou fastest, anoint thine head, and wash thy face; that thou appear not unto men to fast, but unto thy Father which is in secret..."* (Mt. 6:17,18)

These words indicate Jesus expected His followers to fast. He did not want them to do it for show, but for power. His intent was not to prohibit fasting, but to promote the proper aspects of fasting.

SOME RULES FOR FASTING

There are some guidelines concerning fasting which will help you. Please consider:

1. Set aside a definite day of the week or month when you will fast.

2. Observe a special fast in regard to a specific occasion such as a need in your life, in the life of a friend, a special event in your church, special problem facing our nation, etc.

3. Devote as much time as possible to the study of the Bible and of Christian literature during your times of fasting.

4. Decide today to soon devote yourself to a time of fasting and prayer. Fasting is for you and you should be fasting. Discover the power of this spiritual discipline.

How Does God Heal Today

"Have you ever seen a miracle?" What is your answer? What is your immediate response?

I often ask this question when I am teaching a group concerning healing. Most of the people in the groups respond that they have never seen a real miracle.

This negative response reveals to me that they have two basic misconceptions concerning miracles.

MANY CHANNELS

First, it shows they do not appreciate the fact that the Lord uses many channels to bring about His miracle of healing.

Second, it illustrates they do not comprehend that every healing is a miracle regardless of the channel used.

I cannot emphasize enough the eternal truth that the Lord is in the healing business. He uses all kinds of methods. However, the healing is always from Him.

My friend, Dr. Frank Bateman Stanger in his booklet, *"Would You Be Made Whole?"* lists the seven ways of healing which were written by E. Stanley Jones many years ago. They are below and deserve your careful attention.

SURGEONS

God heals through surgeons. Medical history is replete with cases where individuals have received restored health as a result of an operation.

PHYSICIANS

God heals through physicians. God has laid up in nature various remedies which medical science has or is in the process of discovering. However, medicines are to be used wisely and never over-used or abused.

MENTAL SUGGESTIONS

God can heal through mental suggestions. An individual can dwell mentally upon sickness to the point that he will become ill. On the other hand, he can think health, and discover that this aids the healing process. Many times the process of healing has been aided by constructive mental, emotional, and spiritual attitudes.

CLIMATE

God can heal through climate. Although this can be overstressed — for the real climate of health or ill health is within a person — nevertheless some climates are more conducive to health than others.

Individuals plagued with respiratory problems often find the dry climate areas to be much more healthful than high humidity areas.

DELIVERANCE

The Lord heals through an individual's deliverance from underlying fears, loneliness, self-centeredness, purposelessness, resentments, guilts, etc. which produce and prolong illness.

SPIRIT OF GOD

The Lord heals through direct operation of the Spirit upon the body. There are physical healings beyond the explanation of science. In fact, there is no nerve or tissue of your body which is beyond the healing touch of the Lord.

The Lord's arm is not shortened in this scientific and technological age. He is Lord of your whole being — body, soul, and spirit.

RESURRECTION

The Lord heals through the final cure — the resurrection of the body. Some diseases must await the final and complete cure in the resurrection of the body.

In the meantime He supplies sufficient grace for you. Grace not only to bear your suffering, but to use it to His glory until the final release.

CONCLUSION

The Living God does work in and through all of the above. If you realize this you can truly say that you have seen many, many miracles. Thank the Lord for them.

Spiritual Healing — A Personal Witness

I am often asked how I became involved in the Spiritual Healing Ministry. I shall seek to give some background concerning my pilgrimage.

MY FIRST HEALING SERVICE

It was the third Wednesday of May 1959 that I conducted my first public healing service. I began at a time when the crisis of severe illness was upon me.

I could hardly walk. My legs were wrapped each day in elastic stockings to keep them from swelling. I couldn't even turn over in bed without hooking my one leg over the edge of the bed and pulling myself over. I was in constant pain throughout my entire body and was getting progressively worse. This physical problem was affecting me emotionally and spiritually.

It was while so seriously ill that I felt led of the Lord to begin conducting public healing services. I had not read a book on healing, nor attended a healing conference or mission. I simply felt that in obedience I should begin a healing service and trust the Lord for His healing.

In addition to all my other physical ailments, I developed a serious stomach disorder. The doctor put me on a bland diet and told me I could not eat raw fruit or vegetables.

The Lord had other plans for me than an illness that was crippling me. My healing was not instantaneous, but over a period of time the Lord completely healed me.

My aching body was healed and I never had to continue the monthly shots which the doctor said I would have to take the rest of my life.

Instead of being unable to walk I have become a jogger and achieved the ability to jog five miles a day. I have eaten bushels of fruits and vegetables and praise the Lord for His healing.

ALMOST DEFEATED

A few months after I started the healing services, I was almost defeated. Satan discovered a weak spot and almost succeeded in using it in discouraging and defeating me in the area of Spiritual Healing.

His approach was, *"How can you conduct a service of healing and tell people the Lord can heal when you are so ill yourself?"* The Holy Spirit countered with, *"Do you present a perfect plan of salvation?"* I replied, *"Yes I do."* His next question was, *"Are you perfect?"* I acknowledged I was not. The Spirit replied, *"True, Christ alone is perfect. He is the Saviour. You are only the proclaimer of the Good News. Christ does the saving."*

Then the Spirit went on to reveal to me the following insights: *"The Lord is asking you to believe His word and to proclaim the message of healing. You are not the healer. The Lord is not dependent upon your perfection as far as His willingness and power to heal is concerned. Your perfection is not the source of power. Christ is the healing power."*

It was then that I concluded I would conduct services of healing regularly and faithfully even if I had to do so from a wheel chair. However, I praise the Lord that He saw fit to wonderfully heal me.

TO EVERY CHURCH

It was in the spring of 1970 that the Lord gave to me the vision that I should take the message of Spiritual Healing to all of the churches of our nation. This is a tremendous task and great challenge. I realize it won't be easy. I sometimes get discouraged. I am often misunderstood in my efforts and motives. However, the same Lord who healed me in body and soul will provide the way for me to fulfill His desires for my life. I don't have all the answers, but I know the One who is the Answer.

I close by quoting from page 200 of my book, *"Creative Churchmanship." "We know not the end of what we begin, but we know Him who is the beginning and the end. We know not what opposition we shall encounter, but we know what inner strength we have found. We do not choose to look back and become a pillar of salt, but to look ahead and to be the salt of the earth."*

Advent and Healing

Advent means coming or arrival. Advent is the beginning of the ecclesiastical or Church year. It includes the four Sundays preceding Christmas.

Advent speaks of Christ coming as a Babe in the manger. It also reminds us of His coming again as Lord of Lords and King of Kings.

Advent powerfully proclaims that Jesus is coming to each believer as a Source of help and healing.

I suggest that the letters for the word Advent be considered as follows:

A

Accept the truth that the Lord wants you to be whole. It is the perfect season of the year for you to receive God's gift of wholeness of body, mind, and spirit. He desires that you have and live the abundant life.

"I am come that you might have life, and that you might have it more abundant." John 10:10

D

Declare your faith in the Lord and His healing power. You are not the healer, but you have been called to proclaim the good news that Christ is.

V

Visualize the healing for which you are praying. Lift yourself and your loved ones up into the light and love of the Lord. Seek to get your eyes off your problems and unto the Problem Solver.

E

Enlist others in the ministry of healing. You and I need to discipline others in the proven ways of a fruitful ministry of healing.

Each of us must enlist others. No one person can do it all. The following plainly illustrates that one person can never reach the world with the message of wholeness.

"However, even if I were to speak to 1,000 people every night and could convince the 1,000, it would take me five hundred years to speak to everybody now living in the US, and I would go behind at the rate of 2½ million a year due to the continuing population increase. If, on the other hand, I were to speak to one person a week and could convince, inform and instruct that person, and if we each convinced, informed and instructed another person the following week, and the four of us each enlisted another the following week, by this process everyone in the world could be reached in less than twelve months."

N

Number your blessings of this past year. The Lord has been gracious to you. He knows you cannot possibly remember all of His blessings. However, He asks that you not forget them all either. See Psalm 103:1-5.

T

Thank the Lord for His presence and power. Especially give thanks for His many promises upon which you have relied this past year.

Also, thank Him for His promises which give you hope as you face the future. Consider the following thoughts and concepts:

Faith leads to victory in Jesus. (I Cor. 15:57)

The Lord's comfort is always available to all who call. (II Cor. 1:3-5)

The Lord is your Source of healing, material necessities, spiritual strength, and all of your other needs. (Phil. 4:19; I Cor. 3:21)

There is no trial or temptation which can defeat the believer who keeps close to the Lord. (II Cor. 12:9) Believe Him today!

The Economy and Illness

There is full evidence of our living in a very sick world. Headlines blare the news of inflation, unemployment, yes even depression. Where does the message of healing enter this picture?

May I suggest that the message of healing is needed as never before. We must get out the message of the Lord's concern for the whole person. Consider the following:

Dr. M. Harvey Brenner of John Hopkins University has written the book, **Mental Illness and the Economy**. He cites some fascinating and challenging facts for all who are involved in seeking the healing of the whole person.

FINANCIAL STRESS

The concerned Christian must be aware of the fact that financial woes increase the amount of stress which an individual must endure. This stress ultimately issues forth in various forms of illness.

Dr. Brenner points out that the first wave of deaths follow a recession by three years with a second wave coming five to seven years after a recession. This delay results from the time it takes for heart disease to cause death. Kidney failure deaths generally lag behind an economic downturn, while deaths caused by strokes follow a recession by two to four years.

It is obvious that individuals experience increases in the major risk factors during times of economic crises. Some of the risk factors are high blood pressure, increased levels of cholesterol, and increased smoking and alcoholism.

SOURCES OF STRESS

The main sources of stress during economic crises are:

a. the struggle for the basic necessities of life — food, shelter, health care, education for children, and so forth.

b. the loss of ego satisfaction and social standing, and being forced to survive on savings, and/or welfare and unemployment insurance.

c. more drinking and smoking. Strange but true, that when individuals can least afford it financially, they turn to drugs of tobacco and alcohol.

These added stresses add up to increases in suicides, murders, traffic accidents, and to a significant increase in admissions to mental hospitals. Dr. Brenner notes that even infant mortality is related to economic downturns. This is generally because the mother succumbed to the stresses of recessions with increased blood pressure and frequently with doing more smoking and drinking. As a result, she gives birth to a baby that could not survive.

NEGLECT NOT HEALING

Now, considering the above, can any of us neglect the ministry of healing? Indeed not! May I suggest some tangible steps for you:

1. Develop a deeper devotional life.
2. Constantly look to the Lord as the Source of supply for your every need. Your company, the government, others are not the Source of supply. They may be the Lord's instrument, but are not the Source of supply for meeting your needs.
3. Remain firm in your faith that the Lord is with you and will supply your needs. Consider: Ps. 27:1-13,14; 46:1; Phil. 4:19; II Peter 5:7.
4. Reach out to others with your prayers and possessions. Consider: Mt. 25:31-46; Luke 18:1; I John 3:16-18.
5. Faithfully participate in a healing service and the many facets of the ministry of healing.

Patterns of Prayer

The Bible plainly teaches that prayer is not to simply equip a person to do the work of the Church. It teaches that prayer is the work of the Church.

Isn't it interesting that the only specific responsibility of Elders, as listed in the scriptures, is to pray for the sick and to anoint them? What was considered primary to the leaders of the early church has been relegated to almost last place by the contemporary church or completely ignored.

You and I are called to a deep and abiding communion with the Living Lord. Please consider the following scripture.

BELIEVING PRAYER

Mt. 13:58 — "He did not many mighty works...."

Mk. 16:17 — "These signs shall follow those that believe...."

John 14:12 — "He that believeth on me, the works that I do...."

James 5:15 — "The prayer of faith shall save the...."

EXPECTANT PRAYER

Mt. 8:8 — "Speak the word only and...."

Mt. 9:21 — "If I but touch...."

ACCEPTING PRAYER

Mt. 14:36 — "As many as touched...."

PRAYER OF THANKFULNESS

John 11:41 — "...Father, I thank thee that thou...."

PRAYER OF PRAISE

Mt. 15:31 — "...And they glorified the God of Israel...."

PRAYER OF CONFESSION

Rom. 10:9 — "If thou wilt confess...."

James 5:16 — "Confess...pray...that ye may be healed."

I John 1:9 — "If we confess our sins...."

PRAYER OF ABSOLUTION

Rom. 10:13 — "Whosoever shall call...."

I John 1:9 — "...He is faithful and just to forgive...."

PRAYER OF RELINQUISHMENT

Mk. 14:36 — "...Not what I will, but what thou wilt...."

Lu. 23:46 — "...Father, into thy hands...."

Acts 7:59 — "...Lord Jesus, receive my spirit...."

PRAYER WITH LAYING ON OF HANDS

Mk. 6:5 — "He laid hands on few...."

Mk. 16:18 — "...and they shall lay hands on the sick...."

PRAYER WITH ANOINTING

Mk. 6:13 — "...and anointed with oil many who were ill...."

James 5:14 — "...anointing him with oil...."

INTERCESSORY PRAYER

Lu. 22:32 — "I have prayed for thee...."

John 17:9 — "I pray for them...."

Eph. 1:16 — "...making mention...in my prayers...."

PETITIONARY PRAYER

Lu. 18:13 — "...be merciful to me...."

James 5:13 — "..and let him pray...."

A Pattern of Prayer

I am frequently asked, *"How do you pray for someone who is ill?"* This is a very pertinent question and one I shall seek to answer.

I Cor. 12:9 speaks of the gift of healing. I like Dr. William Barclay's insights concerning this verse. *"The church never altogether lost this gift of healing; and one of the biggest things that is happening today is that the Church is rediscovering it. The old Frenchman Montaigne, one of the wisest writers who ever wrote, said about a boy's education, 'I would have his limbs trained no less than his brains. It is not a mind we are educating nor a body; it is a man. And we must not split him in two.' For too long the Church has split man into a soul and a body, and has accepted responsibility for his soul but not for his body. It is one of the great recoveries of our time that once again we are learning to treat man as a whole, and the day will come when the doctor and the minister will once again work hand in hand."*

IMPORTANCE OF PRAYER

I feel to properly answer the above important question, I must first stress the importance of prayer.

It is my firm conviction that prayer is the work of the church. It is not simply a tool to be used to equip a person to do church work. Believers are workers together with God and not for God. See I Cor. 3:9.

After decades of living the Christian life it was Dr. Albert E. Day who said, *"This half-century of pilgrimage has wrought deeply into my soul the conviction that the life of prayer is the most indispensable aspect of our career on earth. Without it, there cannot be either the personal holiness or social effectiveness for which earnest persons yearn and in which alone is there hope for a desirable future for mankind."*

Dr. Alexis Carrel wrote, *"The influence of prayer on the human mind and body is as demonstrable as that of the secreting glands. Its results can be measured in terms of increased physical buoyancy, a greater intellectual vigor, moral stamina, and deeper understanding of the realities underlying human relationships. Properly understood, prayer is a mature activitiy indispensable to the fullest development of personality — the ultimate integration of man's highest faculties."*

An unknown author has succinctly stated, *"Of all the calls flung out across the world the sovereign summons is to intercession."*

A PATTERN

Having established the importance of prayer, may I suggest an approach for you which I use when ministering unto others with prayer.

I. QUIET

The first thing I suggest is to quiet yourself and the one for whom you pray.

II. LIFT

I suggest that in your mind and heart you lift yourself and the one for whom you pray into the light and love of the Lord.

III. VISUALIZE

May you seek to visualize wholeness for the one for whom you are praying. Visualize the Lord's wholeness being transmitted from Him through you to the one for whom you pray.

IV. BELIEVE

Seek to really believe that the spirit of the Lord is at work with you. Believe He will meet the needs of the one for whom you pray.

V. PRAISE

Give thanks to the Lord for His healing which is taking place.

VI. TRUST

Leave the results up to the Lord and maintain your confidence in Him.

A Pattern of Prayer - Quiet

My *Pattern of Prayer* is not a perfect plan of prayer, but I have found it very helpful. I want to present further insights concerning the six steps of the plan.

QUIETNESS

Most believers discover that prayer is a quieting force in their lives. They feel William James was correct when he said, *"The exercise of prayer, in those who habitually exert it, must be regarded by us doctors as the most adequate and normal of all the pacifiers of the mind and calmers of the nerves."*

Prayer really becomes effective when we learn to quiet our whole being in the presence of the Lord before we pray.

I believe the prayer of faith is most often prayed by the relaxed person, and best received by the relaxed person. I do not mean the indifferent, but the relaxed person is one whose confidence is in the Lord.

Dr. A. E. Day writes, *"Right prayer demands a quieting of the whole being...the truest prayer begins when we pass beyond words into deep silence; when lips are hushed; when racing thoughts are stilled; when emotions are placid as the dawning over the waveless ocean."*

The Bible calls for the quiet spirit.

"Be still and know that I am God...." (Ps. 46:10)

"And that ye study to be quiet...." (I Thess. 4:11)

STEPS TO QUIETNESS

You may ask, *"How can a person arrive at this point of holy hush before the Lord? How can I bring others to this place?"* Here is what I do.

When I begin to intercede for another I seek first to quiet my mind. I put forth conscious effort to still the racing mind and to contemplate upon the presence of the Lord. I then seek to quiet my heart and to bring my emotions to a placidity before God. I simply imagine His being with me and giving to me His Peace. Then I seek to quiet my physical body. I consciously imagine every cell of my body being open to His spirit. I desire to be a clear and open channel of His power. I use this approach whether I am ministering to someone present with me or in some distant place. If the person is with me I lay my hands upon them and say the following:

"Now I want you to join with me in this ministry of prayer. I am laying my hands upon you and seeking to quiet my whole being before the Lord. Now I want you to do the same. I ask that to the best of your ability you quiet your mind. Also, I want you to quiet your heart, so that at least for these few moments you will be quiet in the Lord. Let your total emotions relax in the Loving Lord. I want you to seek to relax in your body. Begin at the top of your head and let the relaxed spirit flow through your face, body, legs, to the very tip of your toes. You are now opening yourself completely to the power of the Lord and I am going to minister to you with prayer."

It is amazing to me how many are so tense, and feel they must struggle with the Lord to receive His answer. It is hard for them to realize He is more willing to answer than they are to call.

CONFIDENCE IN THE LORD

I learned a long time ago that the Lord does not hear because we shout or carry on in prayer. In fact, as I searched the Scriptures I discovered it was not the believers who had to shout, but those who worshipped false gods. See I Kings 18:28. Elijah prayed what I have affectionately termed a *"Presbyterian prayer."* It was short and to the point. See I Kings 18:36,37. The fire of the Lord fell and the sacrifice was consumed. Later Elijah learned even more dramatically that the Lord's presence is in quietness. (I Kings 19:12)

A Pattern of Prayer - Lift

The second step in my *Pattern of Prayer* is to lift those for whom you pray into the light and love of the Lord.

THE PROBLEM SOLVER

It is absolutely essential that all of our prayer concerns be lifted unto the Lord. He alone is the Problem Solver.

It is impossible for me to solve anyone's problem or to heal anyone. Only the Lord can do this. His forces of wholeness must be received for any healing or help to come.

Therefore, when I lift someone into the light and love of the Lord, at least for the moment, I get my eyes off of the problem and unto the Problem Solver. If the individual is present when I pray I ask him/her to also imagine being in the light and love of the Lord. Thus together we seek to open all channels for His wholeness to flow.

MY BURDEN BEARER

The Lord is more than willing that you give your burdens to Him. He has asked that you do so.

"Come unto me, all ye that labour and are heavy laden, and I will give you rest." (Mt. 11:28)

"Casting all your care upon Him, for He careth for you." (I Peter 5:7)

WHY LIGHT AND LOVE

I seek to lift myself and others into the light and love of the Lord. I want to bring myself and them to Jesus the Great Physician.

I do not, and cannot, visualize the King of Kings in mere human form. I best picture Him as light and love. This helps me to really realize He is everywhere and able to penetrate every situation. He is willing to bring His touch to every segment of your life.

Thus light and love are parts of the mental picture I need to enable me to lift myself, and those for whom I pray, unto the One who is the Great Physician and the Answer for you.

LIGHT

Light possesses so many beneficial characteristics that it is indeed an appropriate concept concerning our Lord.

Light dispels darkness, reveals, purifies, guides, makes growth possible, serves as a transmitter of voice, is a source of energy, etc.

Light is also the fruit of God's first recorded command. *"And God said, Let there be light; and there was light."* (Gen. 1:3)

Jesus often referred to Himself as light. *"...I am the light of the world: he that followeth me shall not walk in darkness, but shall have the light of life."* (John 8:12)

"I am come a light into the world, that whosoever believeth on me should not abide in darkness." (John 12:46)

There are many Scripture references which refer to Christ as light. *"In Him was life; and the life was the light of men."* (John 1:4)

"To give light to them that sit in darkness..." (Luke 1:79)

"A light to lighten the Gentiles and the glory of thy people Israel." (Luke 2:32)

"But if we walk in the light, as he is in the light, we have fellowship one with the other, and the blood of Jesus Christ his Son cleanseth us from all sin." (I John 1:7)

"And the city had no need of the sun, neither of the moon, ...and the Lamb is the light thereof." (Rev. 21:23)

A Pattern of Prayer - Visualize

Visualize is step three of my *Pattern of Prayer.* I endeavor to visualize wholeness for the one unto whom I minister in prayer.

I seek to visualize the wholeness of the Lord being transmitted through me to the one for whom I pray. The Lord is the Healer. However, as His child I am a channel of His healing power. I am a channel not because I have some very special power to heal, but because I have a very special heavenly Father.

POWER OF IMAGINATION

You have often heard the common appraisal, *"His illness is all in his imagination."* This is possible. Members of the medical profession tell us that a large percentage of illnesses are emotionally induced.

Have you ever dwelled on the fact that you can use your imagination to be well? There is *Emotionally Induced Wholeness* as well as *Emotionally Induced Illness.*

The writer of the book of Proverbs proclaimed a great truth when he said, *"For as he thinketh in his heart, so is he...."* (Pro. 23:7)

Have you ever given time to visualize yourself as healthy, and/or visualize wholeness for the ones for whom you pray?

TANGIBLE HELP

Visualization is a most tangible step to really believing. It puts power into your prayers.

This is the reason I suggest that when you pray for healing for yourself and others, that you visualize them healed. Whatever the illness or situation may be, visualize the Lord bringing His wholeness into the situation.

I know from experience that too often we spend our prayer time dwelling upon the problem. This only compounds the problem.

It was a number of years ago that I discovered this from personal experience. My illness at the time was such that there was no moment of the day that I was not in pain. The only time I was not aware of pain were the brief moments when I was distracted by some activity or conversation. I was constantly praying for the Lord to take away the pain or at least to give me some relief.

I finally realized that my praying for the pain to be relieved was simply concentrating more upon the pain. It was then, and in subsequent years, that I learned to pray for the wholeness which I sought to realize. No longer would I pray, *"Lord, take away my pain."* Now my prayers would be somewhat as follows:

"Father, may your presence prevail in every cell, nerve, and fiber of my being. Thank you for the comfort and the peace and wholeness which you are bringing to me. I bring my total being into your light and love."

This was a completely different and much more helpful approach. Instead of negatively praying for pain to be gone, I positively visualized my body as well. This got my mind off of my pain. I concentrated upon my body as well. I mentally pictured myself free of pain and free to function as I should.

I have since learned to go further and picture myself, or the one for whom I am praying, as using the afflicted organ.

HOW LONG AND HOW OFTEN

You may ask, *"How often and for how long should I visualize wholeness?"* My answer is *"all the time you possibly can."* You will have your weak moments, and slide back into the rut of doubt. However, as much as possible continue to visualize wholeness. A man was on the danger list in the hospital with cirrhosis. I ministered unto him with prayer and visualized the diseased liver cells as whole and the process of deterioration as reversed. I laid hands upon him as I prayed. He had an immediate and remarkable remission. The Lord gave him six more months and he was used to bring several people to Jesus. Prior to this time he had little or no use for the things of the Lord nor for His people.

Effective prayer takes time and practice. The Lord uses the vessel willing to follow His laws and to obey and believe His word. Start where you are to visualize the wholeness of the Lord entering into your situation.

A Pattern of Prayer - Believe

I have presented in detail the first three Steps in my *Pattern of Prayer*; namely Quiet, Lift, and Visualize.

It is in this *Adventure* that I want to consider the Step, *Believe*.

BELIEVE

There are many Bible references which impart the importance of the Step, *Believe*. Please consider

"...he that believeth on me, the works that I do shall he do also...." (John 14:12)

"...all things are possible to him that believeth." (Mark 9:23)

"...for he that cometh to God must believe that He is, and that He is a rewarder of them that diligently seek Him." (Heb. 11:6)

FOR WHOM YOU PRAY

When I pray for someone I endeavor to lead them to really believe that the Lord is present and that He loves them.

This is not always easy to do. Most individuals come to me for prayer because of deep distress. They do not come because of great belief.

I have come to realize that most people come to the Lord initially out of desperation. They do not come because of deep devotion.

Emotionally and spiritually they can no more help themselves than can a seriously physically afflicted person. We who pray for others should realize this problem and face it. May I illustrate?

If you discovered someone on the floor with two broken legs and two crushed arms, you would not insist he get up and phone a physician. You would call the doctor for him. Now many are just as critically crippled emotionally and spiritually. How can prayer enter their situation?

YOU BELIEVE

There is power released when you believe as you minister unto someone with prayer. Jesus honored the faith of others in behalf of a friend.

"When Jesus saw their faith, he said unto the sick of the palsy, Son, thy sins be forgiven thee."

These words found in Mark 2:5 speak volumes.

BELIEVE FOR OTHERS

The Lord does not want you to wait until everyone in the world believes before you pray. He has called you to believe and to pray. Several of the greatest miracles I have witnessed have happened to individuals who had little or no faith.

For instance, I prayed for one who was physically afflicted because of a whiplash, depressed, spiritually dead, and who didn't even want someone to pray for her. Reluctantly she came for prayer ministry with her husband and friends.

She was instantly healed physically, emotionally, spiritually, and received the baptism of the Holy Spirit and the gift of tongues. Quite a miracle for one who did not believe and did not want prayer and Laying-on-of-hands. What released the power of the Lord in her life? I believe it was the faith of those of us ministering unto her with prayer.

SHARE YOUR FAITH

I hope you will not feel I am minimizing the faith of the one for whom prayer is offered. I am trying to point out your responsibility even when the other person's faith is weak or absent. May I illustrate?

I was asked to visit a hospital patient. She was the most seriously ill individual I have ever met, who was restored to relatively good health. She was critically ill physically, emotionally, and spiritually. Her treatment included many weeks in the psychiatric ward and at times being shackled to her bed. Screaming and thrashing, she would curse God and man. She did not, and said she could not believe. As graciously as possible I told her that the Lord did care. She remonstrated with, *"I have no faith and I don't and can't believe!* My reply was, *"True, at this moment. However, let my faith undergird you. I believe the Lord loves you and He is going to heal you."*

She was in no condition to have me present the theological implications of her believing. She needed to be undergirded by my faith. Her recovery has been a miracle. She has often mentioned how she was sustained by me and others. She was much too ill to believe on her own. Your faith is important for you and for others.

A Pattern of Prayer - Praise

Praise is the fifth Step in my *Pattern of Prayer.* Praise is a necessary ingredient of an effective ministry of healing in your own life and in the life of a congregation.

Praise contributes to the development of a climate of healing. It sets the stage for victorious faith. It opens wide the channel to the Lord and keeps the channel open.

THE PLACE OF PRAISE

It is relatively easy to praise the Lord when a healing has occurred. Frequently I am asked what I do for those for whom prayer is offered and there is no healing. My answer is that I seek to lead all people to praise the Lord. All of us need to praise the Lord regardless of what happens at the moment of prayer or what happens in the future.

Most of the healings I witness are not instantaneous. Healing is more of a pilgrimage than it is an incident. This is not to deny the validity of instantaneous healing, but to face the reality that most healings are gradual.

Thus, once I have ministered to an individual for healing I begin to encourage him/her to praise the Lord for the healing which is taking place. This delivers myself and the one for whom I am praying from continually *"begging"* the Lord for healing. It keeps individuals from dwelling upon their illness.

I believe the Lord knows the need and wants to meet your need. Thus, you are to praise Him for doing so and to put your trust in His wisdom and timing.

Many individuals attend healing services week after week and are not necessarily healed of their crucial problem of body, soul or spirit. Even if they are never healed in some areas they are urged to develop a spirit of praise. This will change their entire outlook upon the Lord, their problem, and their prayer life.

Those who develop a spirit of praise soon discover they have moved to a vital and positive life of prayer.

BENEFITS OF PRAISE

The first person benefited from a life of praise is the one who is ill. He may not be healed in the area for which he first prays. But he will be healed in other areas. A good example of this is the person who came to me with great pain and physical discomfort. He developed a spirit of praise and although not cured physically, became a confident, rejoicing child of the Lord.

Another individual as he suffered through what proved to be an incurable physical disease said, *"I can now praise the Lord. Thanks be to Him for what He has done for me on the inside."*

Praise moves from our self-pity parties to times of rejoicing and victory. Murmurings and grumbling always turn inward and do harm to the one complaining. Consider the following:

"Caesar's servants prepared a great feast for his nobles and friends. It was such a terrible day that the whole affair had to be cancelled. In a rage Caesar ordered his archers to shoot their arrows into the heavens at Jupiter, their chief god, to express anger at him for the horrible rainy weather. Of course, the arrows did not reach heaven, but all came right back to earth. A number of them hit archers and wounded many and killed some of them."

Murmurings have only one direction to go and that is back upon the one murmuring. Surely the Lord doesn't want them nor will He receive them. It is our praises which reach beyond us and keep us aglow for the Lord. It is with the sacrifices of praise that the Lord is well pleased. (Heb. 13:15; I Pet. 2:9)

The second way praise is beneficial is that it blesses others. Someone has said, *"If Christians would praise the Lord more the world would doubt Him less."*

If you want to become powerful in prayer then become faithful in praise. *"The fragrant flower of thanksgiving, which blossoms in the heart of God's people, is the result of a little bud called praise which is firmly affixed to the stem and stalk of Christian faith."*

HOW DO YOU PRAISE THE LORD?

There is no "one" way to praise the Lord. However, I offer the following suggestions.

1. Keep your mind on the Problem Solver and often say, *"Praise you Jesus."*
2. Read or recite from memory Scripture which praises the Lord. (Ps. 33:2; 67:3; 100; 103:1,2; 105:1,2; 106:1; 107:1; 117:1,2; 118:1,2; 147:1)
3. Actually say aloud many times during the day, *"Praise the Lord."*
4. Praise the Lord for His victories and benefits. Keep your mind off of the apparent failures. We are not called to be beggars toward God, but to be His children who praise Him continually.

A Pattern of Prayer - Trust

Trust is the last *Adventure* in the series concerning my *Pattern of Prayer*. An understanding of trust is so important.

Frequently I hear individuals say, *"God never seems to hear my prayers or pay attention to me even though I really believe and really trust in Him."*

I can appreciate their feelings, but I cannot appreciate their conclusions. Their comments reveal that they are not really letting things in the hands of the Lord. True trust cannot be a transient or momentary experience.

WHAT IS TRUST?

The dictionary definition of trust is *"to repose; trust in; rely upon; to commit to or as to the care of another with assurance; to put something in the care or keeping of; entrust."*

Anyone who, in a sense, computerizes his petitions to the Lord and then endeavors to keep track of how many he thinks are answered and how many he feels are not answered is making a mockery of prayer.

Believers are called to be committed followers who fellowship with the Lord. They are not cold calculators who keep track of positive and negative responses to their prayers. Prayer is an experience of fellowship with the Lord. It is not a means of using the Lord for your own selfish ends.

A little blind girl was taken from her father's arms by one of his friends. She showed no fear whatsoever. The father was a bit surprised and said, *"Aren't you afraid my child?"* She replied that she was not. He father said, *"But you don't even know who has you."* The little girl's answer is classic and so beautifully conveyed trust as she responded, *"No, but you do father."*

WHENCE COMETH TRUST?

Trust is of the Lord. He imparts a spirit of trust to you as you place your trust in Him. It is as if you must trust, before you are given trust. You are given trust in order that you might trust. I like the words of Andrew Murray: *"Never try to arouse faith from within. You cannot stir up faith from the depth of your heart. Leave your heart and look into the face of Christ; and listen to what He tells you about how He will keep you."*

The Scriptures are so plain as to Whom you should trust with all your heart.

"It is better to trust in the Lord than to put confidence in man." (Ps. 118:8)

"Trust in the Lord with all thine heart; and lean not unto thine own understanding." (Pro. 3:5)

See also Isa. 26:4 and Isa. 26:3.

HOW DO WE TRUST?

Trust is really leaving things in the hands of the Lord. Prayer is no more than vain verbalization if the element of trust is absent. The Lord is the One who must make the ultimate decisions concerning our prayers.

Frequently my disappointments in prayer have turned out to be great blessings. I may not have seen the hand of the Lord in the apparent answer. I certainly beheld the will of the Lord in the ultimate answer.

Psalm 73 is my kind of Psalm. The Psalmist pilgrimage is my pilgrimage. How I love verse 23, *"Nevertheless I am continually with thee; thou hast holden me by my right hand."*

I believe that eternity will reveal a life pattern for each of us which will have been to the Lord's glory. As you minister to yourself and to others may you keep this thought in mind. May you trust the Lord in all things and in all ways. Consider the following as you learn to trust the Lord.

1. Don't get up tight when you pray for others. Trust the Lord. You are not the healer. He is. May you look only unto Him and encourage others to do the same.

2. Leave the results of your prayers in the hands of the Lord. Many feel the Lord's reputation is at stake and thus they frantically seek to immediately see everyone whole. The Lord's reputation is not at stake. He is Lord and always will be. Deep down you know it is your reputation you are concerned about and apparent failure defeats you. Your real calling is to be obedient and to let the ultimate results up to the Lord.

3. Maintain your confidence in the Lord regardless of the circumstances of life. Many live a life of defeat and despair. They are as the one who wrote, *"I entered this world in lowliness; I have lived it in anxiety; I shall leave it in fear."* What a pathetic way to live and die. I like the prayer of the fishermen of Brittany, *"Keep me my God; my boat is small and the ocean wide."* *The Living God* is with you always. (Mt. 28:20)

Stress

Stress is one of the most prevalent characteristics of our day. It seems that all of us are living under a great deal of it all the time.

Stress Chart

Rank	Life Event	Mean Value
1	Death of spouse	100
2	Divorce	73
3	Marital separation	65
4	Jail term	63
5	Death of close family member	63
6	Personal injury or illness	53
7	Marriage	50
8	Fired at work	47
9	Reconciliation with mate	45
10	Retirement	45
11	Change in health of family member	44
12	Pregnancy	40
13	Sex difficulties	39
14	Gain of new family member	39
15	Business readjustment	39
16	Change in financial state	38
17	Death of close friend	37
18	Change to different line of work	36
19	Change in number of arguments with mate	35
20	Mortgate over $10,000	31
21	Foreclosure of mortgage or loan	30
22	Change in responsibilities at work	29
23	Son or daughter leaving home	29
24	Trouble with in-laws	29
25	Outstanding personal achievement	28
26	Mate begins or stops work	26
27	Begin or end school	26
28	Change in living conditions	25
29	Revision of personal habits	24
30	Trouble with boss	23
31	Change in work hours or conditions	20
32	Change in residence	20
33	Change in schools	20
34	Change in recreation	19
35	Change in church activities	19
36	Change in social activities	18
37	Mortgage or loan less than $10,000	17
38	Change in sleeping habits	16
39	Change in number of family get-togethers	15
40	Change in eating habits	15
41	Vacation	13
42	Christmas	12
43	Minor violations of the law	11

Do little things upset you as never before?

Do you feel overly worthless and doubt your own capabilities?

Are you plagued with unexplainable anxieties?

Does practically every situation look hopeless to you?

WHAT IT IS

Stress may be defined as that condition or state when you are ill at ease. It is when the body is not in a state of healthful equilibrium. It is the rate of wear and tear on your body.

A BANK ACCOUNT

I like the way Dr. Hans Salye likens each life to a bank account. He says your vitality has been inherited. You cannot add to it, but you can take from it. Stress accelerates withdrawal of one's vitality.

CONSEQUENCES OF STRESS

Among the many consequences of excessive and prolonged stress are headaches, high blood presure, stomach trouble, general feeling of tiredness, irritability, withdrawal, change in personality, etc.

STRESS CHART

Dr. Thomas Holmes and Dr. Minoru Masuda of the University of Washington in Seattle have given much time to the problem of stress and its consequences. They conclude that good or bad changes in your life affect your body. They developed a Stress Chart to rate the amount of stress caused by events in your life. As you review their Stress Chart and appraise your life, keep in mind that they are presenting only a guideline. The degree of stress and accompanying reactions will vary much from person to person and the Stress Chart can only present a statistical average. Events of the past year or two should be used to comprise your total score.

1. If your score is between 150-199 you are in a mild life crisis.
2. If 200-299 you are in a moderate life crisis.
3. If over 300 you are in a major life crisis.

WARNING SIGNS

Along with the above Stress Rating Scale you may want to consider the following to determine if you are now living under excessive stress.

Do you notice undue tenseness in your body — tense head or neck muscles, excessive fluttering of eyelids, clinched fingers or toes, irregular or shallow breathing?

Do you find yourself being suspicious of friends and bothered even in familiar places and situations?

Are you having trouble getting along with others of your family and/or friends?

Has life lost its meaning?

Surviving Stress

Hypertension is one of the most prevalent diseases of our day. It may be because of your natural tendency toward high blood pressure.

However, it may be caused to a large extent by the pressures of your life. You would be wise to have your physician check your blood pressure and to follow his advice if control measures are needed.

In addition, the following tangible suggestions have been helpful to many.

ALWAYS WITH YOU

The world is going to be with you always. It is not going to change simply because you worry and fret. It will never be a perfect world. Most things are not going to change as you want, nor will all people change as you might desire. Imperfect as the world may be, it is the best one you will live in this side of eternity. You must learn to live with the stress and tensions of our day.

PURPOSEFUL LIVING

The key to conquering tensions is to discover purpose for living. All else is pretty much in vain if purpose is absent.

Commitment to Jesus Christ will add depth and desire to all areas of your life. He is the One who gives the abundant life.

TALK THERAPY

It is true that *"confession is good for the soul."* It is also good for the body. You will discover that verbalizing what is eating you will bring great relief from emotional indigestion.

It will also bring new insight into your problems. It will often help you to become aware of solutions you would otherwise have missed. An honest heart to heart talk with someone in whom you have confidence is excellent therapy.

ESCAPE

Problems are never solved by escapism. However, to get away from a situation for awhile is often a good thing. Tensions at home, office, school, etc. need balanced with time away from them. This enables you to catch your emotional breath. You see yourself and your situation from a different perspective.

PHYSICAL ACTIVITY

It is surprising how different your situation will appear after a game of tennis, a long walk, or some hours in the garden, or after scrubbing down walls.

It is better that pent-up emotions be released through physical activity than through excessive response of your glands.

Dr. Frank Katch of Queens College in New York reports concerning women in his classes who are running up to a half hour a day. *"...their stamina is up, their weight is down and their pride of accomplishment is terrific."*

PLAN YOUR WORK

What do you do when the magnitude of your responsibilities staggers you? A positive response would be to list the tasks which you must accomplish. Place priorities upon each and seek to accomplish them one by one in order of priority. Keep your list and goals within reason. Superman exists only in the comic book. You are limited in strength, knowledge, talent and time. Accept your limitations and set *"possible"* goals for yourself.

LIVE AND LET LIVE

Honestly appraise your own abilities and at the same time be charitable toward others. Many keep themselves in constant turmoil because they expect too much of others.

May you resist the temptation of trying to make others over to suit yourself. Seek to live to the glory of God and to the fullest. Give others the opportunity to do likewise. The overly critical person will become an overly tense person.

WILLING TO BE LOVED

It is intriguing to me that many seek desperately to be loving, but are unwilling to be loved. Even their good works and kind words serve as instruments to keep others at arms length. You will discover relief from many tensions if you are willing to receive the love and warmth of others.

RE-CREATION

Everyone needs to be re-created from time to time. Recreation comes into proper perspective when it is viewed as re-creation. Two individuals were given the assignment of lifting a few ounces with their index finger. One did it constantly and was finally unable to go on. The other rested after every three lifts. He could have gone on for years. Even Jesus took time to pause from the grind of life. See: Mk. 1:35; 6:46; Lu. 5:15,16; 6:12; 9:18.

Defeating Depression

I am appalled at the number of Christians who are living in an almost constant state of depression. It seems that depression is reaching epidemic proportions even among believers.

The suggestions I offer for defeating depression may sound simple, but I sincerely believe they are worthy of your careful consideration.

DEPRESSION

The definition of depression is, *"the act of depressing, or the state of being depressed; low spirits or vitality; dejection, melancholy."*

The depressed individual feels unhappy, useless, without purpose in life, and almost to the place of wondering if they can go on with life.

INWARD

Depression comes from within and not from without. No amount of water can sink a ship until it gets on the inside. In like manner, no circumstance in life can really defeat and depress until you permit it to overwhelm you within.

John Ford put it very well when he wrote, *"Melancholy is not, as you conceive, indisposition of body, but the mind's disease."*

COMMIT

You must come to see that the problem of depression which you have within, must be dealt with by the only One who can really reach within the deepest recesses of your heart.

I would pray you will turn to the Lord in full reliance upon His desire and power to save, sustain, and to satisfy.

You may say, *"I have already committed my life to the Lord."* If you are deeply depressed I would urge you to review your life and heart. Seek to determine if your commitment is of the heart or principally of the intellect.

"Trust in the Lord with all thine heart; and lean not unto thine own understanding." (Pro. 3:5) See: Isa. 20:3; Mk. 9:23; John 14:27.

Above all else you will want to see Jesus. It is reported that when Leonardo da Vinci had finished painting *"The Last Supper"* he invited all his students to see it. They gasped a chorus of *"Ohs"* and *"Ahs."* The students then began to look at the exquisite lace table cloth which was the product of their master's genius. They all spoke to him about it. Leonardo reached for his brush, dipped it in his paints, and with one full stroke wiped out the lacework. He then turned to his students and said, *"You fools, look at the Master's face."*

GOD'S PLAN

Believe me when I say the Lord desires wholeness and joy for you. Jesus gives abundant life.

"I am come that you might have life." (Jn. 10:10) Force your mind into sunshine thoughts. Do this especially when your mind starts the *"instant replays"* of old fears and depressive thoughts. Glen Clark wrote so beautifully of God's Plan. It is as follows:

> God has a plan for me. It is hidden within me, just as the oak is hidden within the acorn, or the rose within the bud. As I yield myself more fully to God, His Plan expresses itself more perfectly through me. I can tell when I am in tune with it, for then my mind and heart are filled with a deep inner peace. This peace fills me with a sense of security, with joy, and a desire to take steps that are a part of the Plan.
>
> God's plan for me is a perfect part of a larger Plan. It is designed for the good of all and not for me alone. It is a many-sided Plan and reaches out through all the people I meet. All the events and people who come into my life are instruments for the unfolding of this Plan.
>
> God has chosen those people He wants me to know, to love and to serve. We are continually being drawn to one another in ways that are not coincidental. I pray that I may become a better instrument to love and to serve that I may become more worthy to receive the love and service of others.
>
> I ask the Father within me for only those things which He wants me to have. I know that these benefits will come to me at the right time and in the right way. This inner knowing frees my mind and heart from all fear, greed, jealousy, anger, and resentment. It gives me courage and faith to do those things which I feel are mine to do.
>
> I no longer look with envy at what others are receiving, nor do I compare myself with them. Therefore, I do not cut myself off from God, the Giver of all good things.
>
> God's gifts to me can be many times greater than I am now receiving. I pray that I may increase my capacity to give and to receive for I can give only a I receive, and receive only as I give.
>
> I believe that when I cannot do those things I desire to do, it is because God has closed one door only to leave ajar a better and larger door. If I do not see that door just ahead, it is because I have not seen, heard, or obeyed God's guidance.
>
> It is then that God uses the trouble or seeming failure which may result to help me face myself, and see the new opportunity before me.
>
> The real purpose of my life is to find God within my own mind and heart, and to help my fellowmen. I thank my Father for each experience which helps me to surrender myself to His will. For only as I lose myself in the consciousness of His Great Presence can His Plan for my life be fulfilled.

I would suggest that you read and reread the above Plan. It so beautifully presents insights which will help you grasp the Lord's love and care for you.

Your depression can be defeated. I pray you may believe...with all your heart, mind, and soul. It is the Lord who is your Helper. Turn to Him.

Defeating Depression - Fear

There is no doubt but what depression has reached epidemic proportion in our nation. Granted it is normal to sometimes feel blue and even at moments to be depressed.

However, extreme depression has hit thousands. They find themselves unable to really cope with all the realities of life. Often they do not sleep well, or they feel tired and worn out all the time. Many are bored with life, and perhaps even suffer a loss of desire for food and even sex.

Below are additional suggested tangible steps to combat the dreaded state of depression.

LIST YOUR FEARS

An exercise of immense value to many, and which may be to you, is to write down a list of everything which depresses you. You should be brutally honest and leave none out. You may want to share your list with a friend, or you may choose never to share it. One thing you will discover is that your depression will probably boil down to some area of fear in your life.

WORK ON YOUR FEARS

Begin to work on deleting your fears from your mind and life. You may want to begin with some lesser ones, but do not unduly delay dealing with your worst fear or fears. Claim the promise, *"God hath not given us the spirit of fear, but of power, and of love, and of a sound mind."* (II Tim. 1:7)

FEARS TO JESUS

Jesus is the only one who can really handle your fears. He wants you to give them to Him. Picture your fears as a bag of garbage. You tightly seal the bag and cast it at the feet of Jesus. You may want to audibly pray as you tell Him how you feel about your fears.

Do not become a garbage collector who takes back the garbage which was left with the Lord. *"Cast your every care on the Lord."* (I Pet. 5:7)

The giving of your fears to Jesus means that you are trying to realistically confront them. The Lord is your defender. He can and will help you throw off the shackles of fear in your life.

It is not what you fear which creates the problem. It is the intensity of that fear.

An individual came to our healing service who was plagued with a fear of dogs. This fear kept him depressed and defeated. It was through the ministry of Laying-on-of-Hands with prayer that he was able to give the fear to Christ.

The fear was confronted, defeated, and abandoned. This believer now realizes that the Lord can enter every area of life. Victory was achieved to the glory of the Lord and to his good.

BEHOLD THE GOOD

The creation story stresses that the Lord beheld what He had made and declared that it was good. (Gen. 1:12,15,18,21,31)

If this is true of creation, how much more is it true of the new creation. *"Therefore if any man be in Christ, he is a new creature; old things are passed away; behold, all things are become new."* (II Cor. 5:17)

The Lord's children should develop the habit of seeing something fine and good in all things. You may have to force your mind and emotions to behold the good and you may have to deliberately look for something good in your situation. However, believe me, there is something good, yea, many things good, in your life — right now. Your thought patterns must be changed from the sick and ugly to the well and wholeness concept.

Your accomplishments in this area will be well worth your time and effort.

Positive thoughts of God and His beauty in His creation brings a joy which will help defeat depression.

It is reported that a friend asked Haydn why his church music was almost always of an animating, cheerful, and even festive quality. This great composer replied,

"I cannot make it otherwise, I write according to the thoughts I feel. When I think upon God my heart is so full of joy that notes dance and leap, as it were, from my pen, and since God has given me a cheerful heart, it will be easily forgiven me that I serve Him with a cheerful spirit."

GIVE THANKS

Depression accents the negative and leads you to magnify the ugly events of your day. May you develop the habit of observing and thinking upon the non-ugly events of each day. These may be such simple things as a pleasant clerk, a smile, etc. Give thanks unto the Lord in all things.

Defeating Depression - Inward Look

A recent survey revealed that 15% of Americans aged 18-74 suffer symptoms of serious depression.

Depression now rivals schizophrenia — a mental illness known as *"split personality"* — as the nation's number one mental health problem.

The cause of depression is complex and varies with each person. It may be because of chemical changes in the body, reaction to outside events, unconscious effects of behavior and personal relationships, or of course, a combination of any or all of these things.

I want in this *Adventure* to consider an honest look at yourself as a tangible step toward defeating depression.

INWARD LOOK

A good honest inward look at yourself is important. Are you really in a state of depression or are you simply having a few days of the *"blues?"* The normal reaction to many experiences in life is a feeling of depression. This may come from experiences of disappointments, loss or stress, or from physical or mental exhaustion.

It is sometimes difficult to distinguish between the normal times of temporary depression and the more serious occasions when help will be needed to overcome a depressive state.

The National Association of Mental Health suggests 10 *"danger signals"* of a possible serious state of depression.

You will want to carefully consider the following:

1. A general and lasting feeling of hopelessness and despair.

2. Inability to concentrate, making reading, writing and conversation difficult. Thinking and activity are slowed because the mind is absorbed by inner anguish.

3. Changes in physical activities like eating, sleeping and sex. Frequent physical complaints with no evidence of physical illness.

4. A loss of self-esteem which brings on continual questioning of personal worth.

5. Withdrawal from others, not by choice but from immense fear of rejection by others.

6. Threats or attempts to commit suicide, which is seen as a way out of a hostile environment and a belief that life is worthless. About one in 200 depressed persons do commit suicide.

7. Hypersensitivity to words and actions of others and general irritability.

8. Misdirected anger and difficulty in handling most feelings. Self-directed anger because of perceived worthlessness may produce general anger directed at others.

9. Almost always assuming you are wrong, or responsible for the unhappiness of others.

10. Extreme dependency on others. Feelings of helplessness and then anger at the helplessness.

It is evident from the above that depression is widespread.

I hope you will search your own life to ascertain the depth of any depressive feelings you may have. May I say we have not honestly faced our situation until we have done more than simply analyze. You need to take the positive step of believing the Lord Jesus when He said, *"I am come that you might have...the abundant life."* (John 10:10)

We are not called to always look inward, but to look outward and upward as well.

Defeating Depression - Prayer Partner

This is the concluding *Adventure* in my series concerning *Defeating Depression.* I would suggest you review the previous ones to get the continuity of this series.

One of the most important facts of the life of each Christian is that he/she has the Holy Spirit as a Prayer Partner.

PRAYER PARTNER

It is wonderful to know you are not alone in your struggle with depression. You have a 24 hour a day Prayer Partner. He is the Holy Spirit. (Rom. 8:26)

The defeat of depression must be a team effort and He is the Captain of the team. Begin each day seeking His guidance and take one step at a time. Permit yourself to be molded by His gentle leading. (John 16:13) Thank Him for the healing which will take place in your life today. (I Thess. 5:18)

So many feel they must do everything alone. They evidently are unaware of the presence and power of the Lord. Or perhaps they are neglectful of His presence and desires for their life.

Many believers are like the little boy who tried to move a heavy stone. He could not do it. His father was observing through the window how he pushed, pulled, and even pried with a big board to move the stone. It was all to no avail.

The child came into the house and the father remarked about his being unable to move the stone. He asked if he had tried everything. The boy replied that he had. The father's response was, *"But you didn't ask me to help."* The child's face brightened and together they went out and easily moved the stone. This is a beautiful lesson for the believer because we so often fail to really ask our Prayer Partner to help.

FOLLOW HIS GUIDANCE

Once you begin to rely upon the Holy Spirit then follow the guidance He gives to you. It may be to mentally and emotionally pour His love and blessing upon those who you feel have hurt or misused you. It may be simply to ask someone to forgive you for having borne resentment toward them. It may be placing your nerves in His calm power and presence.

PHYSICAL ACTIVITY

Along with the old saying, *"Confession is good for the soul,"* can be added the statement, *"Physical exercise is good for the soul and body."* Exercise will help relieve tension and make you stronger to resist periods of depression. Tests have shown that after 15 minutes of exercise the electrical activity in muscles declined 20% and continued declining for an hour. A tranquilizing drug, used on the same person, produced very little difference in electrical activity in the muscles. Your exercise period will be enhanced even more if you think of the wonder of the universe, of your body, and of nature around you.

CONCLUSION

In conclusion, may I emphasize that no one has all the answers to defeating depression. However, I hope that the tangible steps I have outlined will prove of help.

I pray you will get beyond constantly taking your own Emotional Quotient (E.Q.). Many are constantly asking themselves if they are happy or depressed, etc. This habit is very destructive. When these negative evaluations enter, your mind develops the desire and ability to mentally or verbally say *"stop."* This is the wholesome maturity for which you have been seeking. You are on the right track when you put a stop to unwholesome thinking.

There are far too many who want to receive before they believe. May you begin now to dwell upon the wonderful change that is taking place within you, even if it is not evident at the moment. The walk of faith is to believe and then to receive.

May you plant the seeds of health by disciplining yourself to display a cheerful spirit. You are only punishing yourself when you remain constantly displaying your depression through actions and looks. May I rephrase an old axiom, *"Laugh and the world laughs with you, be depressed and you are depressed alone."* Self pity is corrosive and saps your vitality as sure as corrosion stops flow of power on the battery terminals.

The Gift of Healing

I was called to the hospital to pray for a man who was in the throes of terminal cancer. One of our Elders, a good friend of his, had paved the way for my visit.

After a few moments of casual conversation, I explained to him concerning the ministry of Laying-on-of-Hands with prayer. He eagerly accepted this ministry.

WARMTH

Following the LOH he lay with his eyes closed for sometime. It was then that he softly said, *"Pastor, I felt a great warmth flow through my body the moment you laid your hand on my head, and it remained all the time you were praying for me."*

Later that day he experienced a vision of the Lord. He saw Christ appear at the foot of his bed and smile at him. He received a peace of spirit beyond description.

Several days later he passed from this life, but he had a wonderful witness of grace. The Lord used this to greatly touch members of his family in a spiritual way.

ELECTRIC SHOCK

On another occasion several of us laid our hands upon a man and were praying for him. We were standing on a tile floor. After we had been praying for a few minutes a sensation like an electric shock went through our hands.

NOT SIGNS

I mention the above incidents because many people feel these are the things that they must experience if the healing message is to be a part of their ministry.

Nothing could be further from the truth. We are not called to seek signs. We are called to serve Christ. He is the Healer. You and I are to be His obedient followers. The outward signs cannot be our measure of effectiveness.

I have been involved in the healing ministry since 1959. I can assure you that instances like the above are very rare. Further, I never seek outward manifestations as confirmation of my calling to the ministry of healing.

GUIDELINES

I believe there are some general guidelines to keep in mind as you begin and continue a ministry of healing.

1. It is true that there are a few individuals with special gifts of healing, just as there are a few with unique gifts of evangelism, etc. But every believer is not an Oral Roberts or Kathryn Kuhlman. Every believer is not a Billy Graham or James Kennedy in the area of evangelism. Would we leave all evangelism or healing ministry to these nationally known leaders? Perish the thought! All believers are called to a life of obedience as much as they are. We can't all be generals. The lowly private is still a vital part of the army.

2. The disciple of the Lord is to go forth with His message of wholeness. (Mk. 6:13; Lu. 10:1-3; 17-20; Acts 8:4-8)

3. Leave the results and outward signs up to the Lord. You are not the Healer. You, nor any one else, are called to change the Lord's mind concerning someone's condition. You are a believer called to always cooperate with the Lord's plan of wholeness for individuals.

4. The gift you are really seeking is the gift of wholeness for the one for whom you pray. It is not the gift of some outward manifestation to prove you are a so called *"healer."*

5. The potential for healing is with every believer. Not because of whom he/she may be. It is because of the One who is the Great Physician and in whose Name you minister. It is He you believe and serve. (Mk. 9:23)

In conclusion, do not wait until you receive some unique sign confirming your healing ministry. Begin this pilgrimage now in the Lord.

Inner Illness

The importance of Inner Healing is appreciated to a greater degree when you have an understanding of Inner Illness. Therefore, I would like to present some insights concerning the causes of Inner Illness.

INNER ILLNESS

The wounds deep within your inner being have been inflicted by many forces and factors. Some of them may be as follows:

1. *Undue concern for your past actions or statements.* You have become deeply concerned that you said or did the wrong thing. You live with almost a constant feeling that you wish you had not said or done a particular thing. You find it impossible to leave your yesterdays with the Lord. You have become a prisoner of your past.

2. *An incident or event may leave a deep impression long after the details are consciously forgotten.* You may have witnessed a tragedy, been involved in a tragedy, or have been badly frightened by some incident or person. An example of this is the individual who had a dread fear of dogs. One day the completely forgotten incident of having been bitten by a dog when very young crossed his mind. A healing took place whch removed this fear.

Dr. Thomas A. Harris in his book, *"I'm OK — You're OK,"* relies on the studies of W. Penfield to support the fact that we are deeply affected by events which may have been consciously forgotten.

"Perhaps the most significant discovery was that not only past events are recorded in detail but also the feelings that were associated with those events. An event and the feeling which was produced by the event are inextricably locked together in the brain so that one cannot be evoked without the other."

Penfield reported: *"The subject feels again the emotion which the situation originally produced in him, and he is aware of the same interpretations, true of false, which he himself gave to the experience in the first place. Thus, evoked recollection is not the exact photographic or phonographic reproduction of past scenes or events. It is reproduction of what the patient saw and heard and felt and understood."*

3. *The hurts of unpleasant relationships.* You may have been treated cruelly by a parent, relative, a friend, or school mates. Perhaps you discovered you were an unwanted child and looked upon as a burden by your parents. Perhaps someone at work may have deliberately said unkind words, or you discovered you were not really needed or wanted by the company.

4. *Your own actions can wound the inner being almost beyond repair.* It may be deeds of dishonesty, immorality, or spiritual disobedience which will take their toll of your inner peace and power.

5. *Some real or imagined physical disorder which becomes a stumbling block to inner wholeness.* The very obese, the extremely short or tall person, an ugly birthmark, pronounced nose, deformed lip, crippled arm or leg, etc., can serve as a source of inner conflict and illness.

An acquaintance of mine would spend hours looking in the mirror at his *"deformed"* nose. He dropped out of college and ultimately ended up being institutionalized in a mental ward. However, in reality his nose was perfectly normal in appearance. He was one of the most handsome men on campus.

6. *The emotional state of your mother prior to your birth.* Strange as it may sound, psychologists now tell us we are affected emotionally even while being carried in the womb. The emotions of the mother can affect the unborn child as directly and deeply as drugs may affect the unborn.

MANIFESTATIONS

The manifestation of inner illness is varied and complicated. However, some of the outward signs of inner illness are as follows:

Aimlessness	*Fear of failure*	*Resentment*
Anger	*Fear of disapproval*	*Sadness*
Anxiety	*Guilt*	*Self-indulgence*
Condemnation	*Hate*	*Self-pity*
Confusion	*Hopelessness*	*Suspicion*
Despair	*Indifference*	*Unbelief*
Despondency	*Inferiority*	*Unforgiving*
Disobedience	*Jealousy*	*Unrighteousness*
Doubt	*Lack of vision*	*Vacillation*
Fear	*Laziness*	*Worry*

HOPE FOR HEALING

You can be delivered from the above through the Inner Healing of your Inner Illness. The following Scripture presents graphically the hope we have in Christ Jesus. *"We are praying too, that you will be filled with His mighty, glorious strength so that you can keep going no matter what happens — always full of the joy of the Lord, and always thankful to the Father who has made us fit to share all the wonderful things..."* (Co. 1:11-14)

Inner Healing Through God's Love

The great need of our day is for Inner Healing. This I state in the presence of much physical distress on every hand.

However, regardless of how devastating a physical affliction may be, it still is not as dreadful as the hell of inner turmoil and conflict.

Betty Tapscott in her excellent book, *"Inner Healing,"* writes, *"Inner healing is the healing of the inner man: the mind, the emotions, the painful memories, the dreams. It is the process through prayer whereby we are set free from feelings of resentment, self-pity, depression, guilt, fear, sorrow, hatred, inferiority, condemnation, or worthlessness, etc."*

I am intrigued with the way the Apostle Paul presented inward victory. *"When you came to Christ he set you free from your evil desires, not by a bodily operation of circumcision but by a spiritual operation, the baptism of your souls. For in baptism you see how your old, evil nature died with him and was buried with him; and then you came up out of death with him into a new life because you trusted the Word of the mighty God who raised Christ from the dead. You were dead in sins, and your sinful desires were not yet cut away. Then he gave you a share in the very life of Christ, for he forgave all your sins, and blotted out the charges proved against you, the list of commandments which you had not obeyed. He took this list of sins and destroyed it by nailing it to Christ's cross. In this way God took away Satan's power to accuse you of sin, and God openly displayed to the whole world Christ's triumph at the cross where your sins were all taken away."* (Col. 2:11-15LB)

BACK TO BASICS

Where do you start with Inner Healing? How does one begin the pilgrimage of spiritual surgery which will bring the Inner Healing so desired and needed?

I believe it comes most frequently with a return to the basic concept of the Lord's love for each individual. One's basic relationship to the Lord is the key to ultimate Inner Healing. Herein lies the solution to sin, sickness, and the feelings of unworthiness.

A person came to me out of deep desperation. He had received counseling from six psychiatrists and several clergy over a period of two decades. He would at times receive temporary relief. However, his nagging inner problems and turmoil continued. He was still living a tormented and defeated life. He had come to me hoping for some help.

It was during the first counseling period that I felt led to discuss with him the basic problem of his relationship to God through our Lord Jesus Christ.

In my opinion, he would never be delivered of inner turmoil until he had come to grips with his relationship with the Lord. I presented the dynamic but simple message of God's love for him and he seemed to change immediately.

I will never forget one of his statements after the reality of the Lord's presence and forgiveness got through to him. He said, *"Why didn't someone explain this to me years ago?"* The Good News was his most urgent need and then further Inner Healing took place. Today he is better.

GOD LOVES YOU

What was the good news which I presented to him? It was simply, *"God loves you."* He was like many I know who try desperately to love God. However, they cannot accept the fact that God loves them. In their own way they are trying to love God and yet feel estranged from the Lord. This creates the situation of love going only one way, and this is devastating.

Some of the most tragic situations I have encountered are those where love goes only one way. I see it with couples when one spouse desperately loves and the other has lost or never had love for their mate. Or with the teenager who feels her parents do not love her, even though in reality they love her very much. The result in the teenager's life is chaos.

Or another example of the frustrations of unreturned love is the high school girl madly in love with the star football player who does not even notice her. Here again love is going only one way and the results are terrifying. Love to be vital and dynamic must be a two way street.

The secret of life is not our frantic efforts to love God, but our humble acceptance of the fact that He loves us. It is reported that the famous Karl Barth was asked, *"What is the greatest truth you have learned from your years of study of Scripture and theology?* His answer, *"Jesus loves me this I know, for the Bible tells me so."*

ACCEPT GOD'S LOVE

The first step to your Inner Healing is to accept God's love for you. He loves you far more than you could ever love Him. Respond to His love. His real love leads to your real life.

Inner Healing - The Memories

You may ask, *"Why the emphasis upon healing of the memories when there is a discussion on Inner Healing? Was not all of this cared for when I came to Jesus and received Him as my Lord and Saviour?"*

Yes, it was cared for by Him. However, many do not realize this. They do not appropriate His healing to every aspect of their lives. Many continue to carry burdens and to suffer emotionally, spiritually, and physically in ways from which they can be delivered.

Just because you are a believer is no reason to automatically expect you will know and understand all spiritual laws. You may own a farm, but this does not necessarily mean you are an excellent farmer. In like manner, you may be a child of the King, but this is not a valid reason to assume you understand everything about His Kingdom. Thus, the healing of the memories is a vast new frontier for most believers.

JESUS IN THE NOW

Any consideration of the healing of the memories necessitates the important truth that Jesus is in the *NOW*. He is and always has been. A simple and yet profound truth is that for Jesus tomorrow will never be and yesterday never was. It is always this moment for Jesus.

"...Before Abraham was, I am." (John 8:58)

"Jesus Christ the same yesterday, and today, and forever." (Heb. 13:8)

INNER HURTS

Many of you carry inner hurts which have long since been forgotten as far as the incident is concerned. But the consequences remain. Many of the hurts are small ones but their accumulative effect is devastating to your emotional and spiritual life.

Some hurts are enormous and leave an immediate and powerful impact from which you may never fully recover. Whatever the magnitude or quantity, the net result is an aching heart and frustrated life. You yearn to have the inner drag removed and your spirit set free.

NEEDED TRUTH

One of the truths you need to really understand and accept is that Jesus is the same yesterday, today, and forever. Most of the inner conflict concerning memories is conquered when this truth is grasped. It is no more difficult for Jesus to heal the past than for Him to heal a present affliction. This truth, once grasped, removes the negative power of the past and the haunting fear of the future.

Jesus can heal any aspect of your memories. He was there when the event occurred. The past is always *NOW* for Him. There is no time to the timeless Jesus. His forgiveness, cleansing, and healing power are manifest in every second of your life. He is always there.

May you use your God given gift of memory to go back through your life and let Jesus heal in all areas. Your mind can prayerfully recall the events of today, yesterday, last week, last month, last year, the past many years, your early twenties, teenage years, Jr. High, elementary grades, kindergarten, pre-school, and the moments of your first conscious recollections.

You can even ask for the Lord's healing to come to the moments of your birth and into all the events surrounding your entrance into the world. He is even in the events when you were in your mother's womb. In other words, all of your life can be engulfed in the healing love of our Lord.

FOR YOU

The healing of the memories is for you. Probably everyone reading this *Adventure* has some area of the memories which needs the healing touch of the Lord. Isn't it good news to know that He can and will heal your memories? He is in the *NOW* of your life — be it yesterday or 80 years ago — that the event took place.

I encourage you to permit Jesus to enter into every area of your past. He will frequently reveal areas of need you had long forgotten. He will bring an awareness which will issue forth into a wonderful healing.

FREE AT LAST

You have permitted Christ to sweep back through your memories. You have asked for His healing in every situation. Now, do not become a garbage collector. Do not gather up all your hurts from whence you have been delivered. You have given your burdens to Him and He is most willing to keep them. He does not want you to have them any more.

"Cast all your care upon him; for he careth for you." (I Pet. 5:7) Please consider the following verses: (II Cor. 3:17; John 8:36)

Some Steps to Inner Healing

We live in a very fast moving and mobile age. A classic example of the mobility of our society and the frantic search for thrills is an event of the Bicentennial year of our nation.

The Concord plane loaded in Texas. Flew to Paris for celebration of New Year's Eve. The new year was greeted in Paris. The plane took off and the passengers celebrated over the Atlantic. Because the plane can travel over 1,300 miles per hour they were able to celebrate again in Washington, D.C.

As exciting as multiple celebrations of the new year may be, it will not bring the wholeness that is needed. A few rich people were able to make this historic journey. However, people of all ages and status in life need to make the Journey to inner wholeness.

IMMOBILIZED

Isn't it a shame that in this mobile day so many are bound and immobile? They are immobilized by the forces of evil and even Satan himself.

Inner healing eludes many even though they so desperately desire it.

YOUR INHERITANCE

Every believer has the inheritance which includes freedom in the Lord. (John 8:36; II Cor. 3:17)

You need not remain a prisoner of your past nor of your future. Jesus is in the *NOW* of your life. Your inner turmoil can be healed through Him.

Howard Hughes, America's richest man, illustrates so vividly the way many of us live spiritually. *TIME* magazine said this about the multibillionaire:

"...a tortured, troubled man who wallowed in self-neglect, lapsed into periods of near-lunacy, lived without comfort or joy in prison-like conditions and ultimately died for lack of a medical device that his own foundation had helped to develop."

Many believers live as helplessly in the spirit. They do not appropriate the power available for the inner healing which is desired. They miss the eternal truths expressed by Paul when he wrote,

"But my God shall supply all your need according to his riches in glory by Christ Jesus." (Phil. 4:19)

STEPS TO INNER HEALING

There are some suggested steps which are very helpful when it comes to receiving inner healing. I list below a few of them.

1. Look only to the Lord for your wholeness — There can be no real release for you and yours through the false gods or the occult. The Lord is your Healer.

"Regard not them that have familiar spirits, neither seek after wizards, to be defiled by them; I am the Lord your God." (Lev. 19:31) See also Deut. 18:9-14.

2. Trust in Jesus Christ only as the giver of freedom, peace and purpose — The basic need of each person is fellowship with the Lord. This can be achieved through Christ and sets the stage for a wholeness within and without. The Scriptures point the way of confession which brings deliverance.

"That if thou shalt confess with thy mouth the Lord Jesus, and shalt believe in thine heart that God hath raised him from the dead, thou shalt be saved." (Rom. 10:9)

"If we confess our sins, he is faithful and just to forgive us our sins, and to cleanse us from all unrighteousness." (I John 1:9)

3. Forgive any and all — God has chosen to limit Himself in some areas. One such area is forgiveness. He says we cannot really be forgiven until we are willing to forgive. Resentfulness is the root of much illness. The inner turmoil of inner resentment will frequently manifest itself in emotional and physical disorders. Plato ages ago is reported to have said, *"All diseases of the body proceed from the mind or soul."*

An unknown author penned the following profound insights: *"Saints are men who permit God's forgiveness to come into them so fully that not only are their sins washed out, but also their very selves, their egos, and the root of their self-will. ...I forgive to the level that I have been forgiven, and if that level is moderate (because ...I wanted only to lose my vices and not myself) I can forgive only people who have offended moderately, and my forgiveness helps them only moderately."*

The only aspect of the model prayer which was amplified by our Lord dealt with forgiveness. (Mt. 6:14,15) Forgive and live!

A Prayer for Inner Healing

There is no magic formula for Inner Healing. However, there are some steps which have helped thousands. One of these steps is to pray a sincere prayer for Inner Healing.

This prayer for Inner Healing is not a perfect prayer. You may desire to revise it to fit your own needs and life situations. Some of the aspects covered in the prayer will not be applicable to you. However, I suggest you pray the prayer and let the Spirit of the Living Christ permeate every facet of your being.

PREPARATION FOR PRAYER

There are some steps which will help prepare you for this prayer. I would encourage you, first of all, to quiet yourself before the Lord. Endeavor to the best of your ability to quiet your mind. Really quiet your mind and try to shut out every thought and focus all on Jesus.

Then seek to quiet your heart or emotions. You can do this for at least a few moments regardless of the distractions in your life or the frustrations you may be facing.

Now move to the quieting of your body from the top of your head to the bottom of your feet.

Now after you have quieted your entire being, keep in mind that the Spirit is going to enter every thought, every emotion, and every cell and fiber of your body. You are open to the forces of healing and help. You rebuke all the forces of unrighteousness and illness.

As you pray, I hope you will appropriate into your present and past life the forgiveness, power and strength of the Lord Jesus.

Many find it most help to pray this prayer out loud.

THE PRAYER

Lord Jesus, I pray that at this very moment I will realize you are receiving me just as I am. You know my every thought of each second of my present and past life.

You know every hurt I have experienced and fear I carry, and every painful memory which haunts me.

You are completely aware of the areas of guilt that leave me defeated.

MY FUTURE

Now Lord Jesus, I want to give to you my future. A future which I often dread and fear because of the pressures and problems of the past as well as the uncertainty of what lies ahead. I ask that you reach into my mind right now in such a way as to take away the fear of the future. Help me to walk into that future fully aware of your power, presence and love.

Enable me to leave the future in your hands, and with confidence I now commit my life to you anew and at greater depth. I know that the peace you give this moment is the same peace I can have in the future. It is your peace. The world did not give it. The world cannot take it away from me. Yes, Lord, I believe as never before that my future is in Your hands.

MY PRESENT

And now Lord Jesus, take these present moments and heal me abundantly. I invite you to come into the areas which weigh heaviest on my heart and mind. Heal my anxiety, enter into the very center of all my present problems, bring wholeness in the midst of my illness, and permeate the lives of those I love with your glory and power. I believe you are in the *NOW* of my life and are bringing just what I need to face each moment and each situation.

MY PAST

And now Lord Jesus, I invite you to heal my memories of the past. The immediate as well as the distant past I bring to you. I pray you will heal my yesterday, my past week, month, and year. In areas where I have failed — please forgive. The troubled areas which cling to my mind and heart I submit to you and ask that you — please cleanse.

I want you to walk through the conscious memory of my working years. Bring your healing to the many hurts, frustrations, and failures of people and positions.

I open to you the years when I left home to establish my own home. During this period heal the scars which developed through relationships with parents, friends, and with spouse. Where there have been resentments, may they be replaced and removed by your Spirit. Where frustrations have left their ugly scars, I turn them all over to you.

I bring my teenage years to you, Lord Jesus. It was a time when I rapidly moved through the trauma of new emotions. There were new fears and a lot of painful memories. Many of the incidents as a teenager left me humiliated and with feelings of guilt. I give these years to you and thank you for the healing you bring to them.

My junior high years come to my mind Lord Jesus. I pray you will move back through them and help me.

Please enter my elementary grade years as I started to go to school. I had so many new things to face and new facts to learn. New faces and many new adjustments.

Lord, I invite you into my preschool years even though I can't consciously remember much about them. Let your healing come and set me free from those things of this period of my life which would hinder fullness of life now.

Jesus, I know you were present at the moment of my birth. Present during the moments of the trauma of my breaking into this strange and terrifying world. May I feel and know your peace surrounding my birth. Please move through the months I was in my mother's womb. May all those moments be bathed in your love and tender care. I want you to be in every emotion of my days from conception to now. I am grateful you have walked with me back through my life. Thank you for your Inner Healing. Amen!

The Bible and Healing

Many believers do not appreciate the power of the Holy Scriptures. They fail to appreciate that they contain the most needed message of our day.

If I were to give you a quart of diamonds they would not be as valuable and practical as a proper understanding of the Word. Diamonds cannot suffice for obtaining and maintaining the spiritual, physical, and emotional health you desire. Many almost literally die grasping for *"diamonds"* when what they really need is to understand the truth of the Holy Bible.

NEW INTEREST

"He is eating better, and we are encouraged. His appetite is returning." These are common statements when one who is ill begins to recover. The desire for food is an indication that health is returning.

In like manner, I feel the great hunger for God's word today is a sign of returning health to many churches. The desire to study the Word at depth is greater today than probably in the entire history of the world. In every nation there are thousands hungering for an understanding of the Bible. New translations of the Book have sales in the millions. Bible study groups are increasing daily. It is a new day for God's people.

IMPORTANCE

How important is the Word? What can we find in the Word to help us for each day we face? The writer of Proverbs tells us that health shall spring forth from the Word when it is rightly received and believed.

"My son, attend to my words: incline thine ear unto my sayings. Let them not depart from thine eyes; keep them in the midst of thine heart. For they are life unto those that find them, and health to all their flesh." (Pro. 4:20-22)

Do not the words speak to us today?

The Bible does not have to remain a closed Book. The Lord wants you to read and to understand.

THE MESSAGE

A careful study of the Word reveals the Lord's deep desire for your wholeness. You discover that the Lord Jesus was revealed for all of your diseases and not simply for your sins. This is a message to be received joyfully and to be understood by every believer.

"...Himself took our infirmities, and bare our sickness." (Mt. 8:17)

"Who his own self bare our sins in his own body on the tree, that we, being dead to sins, should live unto righteousness: by whose stripes ye were healed." (I Pet. 2:24)

"Beloved, I wish above all things that thou mayest prosper and be in health, even as thy soul prospereth." (III John v.2)

ALL YOUR DISEASES

If you were to discover a cure for just one disease you would be heralded as a great scientist. It is a mystery to me that the Word is neglected so much when it presents a message of healing and hope for all diseases. The Old and New Testaments both present the Lord as your healer.

"Who forgiveth all thine iniquities; who healeth all thy diseases." (Ps. 103:3)

"And Jesus went about all Galilee, teaching in their synagogues, and preaching the Gospel of the kingdom, and healing all manner of sickness and all manner of disease among the people." (Mt. 4:23)

Our Lord told us that the message of healing and miracles will continue until the end of the age. *"...he that believeth on me, ...greater works...shall he do."* (John 14:12)

The Bible is not a book of magic, but a book of miracles. It does not present false hope.

Christ's Ministry

The Good News of the Christian faith is that Jesus Christ has come to be the Savior of the world. He has revealed to us the Father's love. He was willing to give His own life for us while were were yet sinners.

How did the Lord and others of His day see this expression of His power and love? How did he tangibly express His desire for salvation *(wholeness)* for individuals of His day and for you and me today.?

You will be encouraged as you consider the emphasis our Lord put upon wholeness of body, soul, and spirit. Please prayerfully consider the following concerning our Lord's ministry.

CHRIST'S OWN APPRAISAL

There are several occasions when Christ refers to His own ministry. He could have said anything He desired. It is interesting to me how many times His summary of His own efforts stressed healing.

1. He chose a passage of healing and hope to explain to those present at the synagogue.

"The Spirit of the Lord is upon me; for the Lord hath anointed me to preach good tidings unto the meek; he hath sent me to bind up the brokenhearted, to proclaim liberty to the captives, and the opening of the prison to them that are bound; To proclaim the acceptable year of the Lord, and the day of vengeance of our God; to comfort all that mourn;..." (Lu. 4:16-24)

2. The Lord's response to the disciples of John included the centrality of healing in His ministry. He did not send John a deep theological or philosophical answer. He said to tell him what He was doing.

"Now when John had heard in the prison the works of Christ, he sent two of his disciples, and said unto him, Art thou he that should come or do we look for another? Jesus answered and said to them, Go and show John again those things which ye do hear and see: The blind receive their sight, and the lame walk, the lepers are cleansed, and the deaf hear, the dead are raised up, and the poor have the gospel preached to them..." (Mt. 11:2-6)

3. Jesus' response to the Pharisees who were concerned that Herod was going to kill him was one of love and power. He wanted Herod to know His ministry included healing the body, soul, and spirit of those who came to Him.

"And he said unto them, Go ye, and tell that fox, Behold, I cast out devils, and I do cures today and tomorrow, and the third day I shall be perfected." (Lu. 13:32)

CHRIST'S ASSIGNMENT

The above speaks of Christ's appraisal of His ministry. Now we consider the assignments He gave to His followers. Isn't it interesting He did not instruct them to form committees or to be expert organizers. He did not even assign them to develop creeds or structures of worship. The following scripture references clearly show what he wanted His followers to do.

1. He chose to give the following assignment to His 12 disciples.

"And when he called unto him his twelve disciples, he gave them power against unclean spirits, to cast them out and to heal all manner of sickness and all manner of disease. And as ye go, preach, saying, The kingdom of heaven is at hand. Heal the sick, cleanse the lepers, raise the dead, cast out devils: freely ye have received, freely give." (Mt. 10:1,7,8)

2. The Lord's assignment to the 70 disciples was for them to proclaim wholeness.

"And heal the sick that are therein and say unto them, The kingdom of God is come nigh unto you. ...And the seventy returned again with joy, saying, 'Lord, even the devils are subject unto us through thy name." (Lu. 10:9,17)

3. The Lord's prediction concerning His future followers was one of great power and wholeness.

"Verily, verily, I say unto you, He that believeth on me, the works that I do shall he do also; and greater works than these shall he do; because I go unto my Father." (John 14:12)

OTHERS APPRAISAL

The above presents how the Lord appraised His earthly ministry. Also, what he expected and does continue to expect from His followers. The below presents what others saw as the outstanding characteristic of His ministry.

1. Herod was not bothered by what Jesus said, but by what He did. He was shaken by the healings of our Lord.

"And said unto his servants, This is John the Baptist; he is risen from the dead; and therefore mighty works do shew forth themselves in him." (Mt. 14:2)

2. Nicodemus was intrigued by Christ because of the power he witnessed issuing forth from our Lord.

"The same came to Jesus by night, and said unto Him, Rabbi, we know thou art a teacher come from God; for no man can do these miracles that thou doest, except God be with him." (John 3:2)

3. Peter's summary of our Lord's ministry was that it was a ministry of healing.

"How God anointed Jesus of Nazareth with the Holy Ghost and with power: who went about doing good, and healing all that were oppressed of the devil; for God was with him." (Acts 10:38)

4. The two on their way to Emmaus felt the Lord's mighty works were known by all. They saw the works as characteristic of the ministry of our Lord.

"And he said unto them, 'What things?' And they said unto him, Concerning Jesus of Nazareth, who was a prophet mighty in deed and word before God and all the people." (Lu. 24:19)

5. The members of the early church witnessed the healing power of the Lord. They wanted the power to flow through them to His glory.

"And now, Lord, behold their threatenings: and grant unto thy servants, that with all boldness they may speak thy word. By stretching forth thine hand to heal; and that signs and wonders may be done by the name of thy holy child Jesus." (Acts 4:29,30)

Christ's ministry of healing is our ministry today.

God's Health Care Plan - Compassion

I meet many people who are deeply distressed and they wonder if God really cares. It is from them I hear statements such as:

"I pray and pray but nothing happens and it is as if God doesn't even hear me."

"I find myself so depressed and I wonder if the Lord loves me and I sometimes find myself thinking terrible things even about God."

"I don't believe God wants me to be well."

"I just feel so lost."

If one of the above fits you today, then it is that I have Good News for you. God does care for you. He wants you to know that He cares. He does have a wonderful health care program for you.

GOD DOES CARE

We hear a lot about a health care program for all of our nation. I feel a most urgent message needed by millions is that the Lord has a health care program.

His program includes wholeness of body, mind, and spirit. He is not simply a powerful Creator who left struggling humanity with no help or hope. He is a loving Father who cares for your health and mine.

A BASIC INGREDIENT

Basic to His health care program is His compassion and mercy. The Word plainly teaches that God does care.

The Lord is gracious, and full of compassion; slow to anger and of great mercy, The Lord is good to all: and His tender mercies are over all His works." (Ps. 145:8,9)

If the Lord cares, which he definitely does, then He is not only able to heal, but he is willing to heal. The Bible imparts more than details of a God of power. It reveals our God of Love. Power infers He is able to do great things, and this is true. Love and mercy revealed through His Word teaches us He is willing to do great things. There is a great difference between being able to do something and being willing to do it. God is able and willing.

Many do not doubt the Lord's power to heal, but often these same individuals will doubt His desire to heal. Is it not as bad to doubt willingness as it is to doubt ability?

You may doubt my ability to do good for you. However, I would be bothered if you doubted my desire to do good for you. I can understand someone saying to me, *"I know you would help me if you could."* It would be terrible if they would say, *"I know you could help me if you would."*

You must bring honor to the Lord by not only believing in His ability, but also believing in His availability. You and I must believe that He is able to heal, and that He is most willing to heal. His health care program is for you.

The heavenly Father's health care program was beautifully accepted and fulfilled in the life of our Lord Jesus. His earthly ministry was one of great compassion. He revealed a Father of mercy and compassion.

"And there came a leper...and Jesus, moved with compassion, ...said, I will; be thou clean..." (Mk. 1:40-45)

"...and Jesus...saw a great multitude, and He was moved with compassion toward them, and He healed their sick." (Mt. 14:13,14)

"And as they departed from Jericho...two blind men...cried out...have mercy...Jesus had compassion...their eyes received their sight..." (Mt. 20:29-34)

God's health care program begins with His very nature. You can no more hold back His mercy than can the flood waters be kept from the crevices of buildings and lands. He is the *"...Father of mercies, ..."* (II Cor. 1:3)

God's Health Care Plan - Love

Your wholeness of body, mind, and spirit is determined to a large extent upon your understanding and application of God's love plan.

Love is one of the vital facets of His health care plan. He desires your wholeness, but expects love to be an avenue to receive and to maintain it. It is the foundation of all that is meaningful and as Swedenborg has said, *"Love in its essence is spiritual fire."*

DOES GOD LOVE?

You may ask, *"Now really, does God love? Does God love me?"* I would answer, *"Do birds fly? Do fish swim? Does the sun rise each day? Do thirsty plants revive with water?"*

You see, the love of God is as natural as the many natural things we daily take for granted. Sure it is impossible to give complete answers to all the suffering in the world. It is also impossible to account for all the goodness and beauty in the world without acknowledging a God of love.

"...God is love..." (I John 4:8,16)

"If ye then, being evil, know how to give good gifts unto your children, how much more shall your Father which is in heaven give good things to them that ask Him?" (Mt. 7:11)

"Greater love hath no man than this, that a man lay down his life for his friends." (John 15:13)

WHEN DOES GOD LOVE?

I feel the problem with many is that they suspect God's love is spasmodic and conditional. They feel that if they are *"good"* and/or *"lucky"* the Lord may occasionally shower them with a dose of His love.

It as if He dispenses His love from a love *"Dropper"* — a precious little drop at a time and very infrequently.

Nothing could be further from the truth. The Lord's love is with you always. He desires wholeness for you because of His love. There is nothing which can come between you and His love.

"...nothing shall be able to separate us from the love of God which is in Christ Jesus our Lord." (Rom. 8:39)

"...while we were yet sinners, Christ died for us." (Rom. 5:8)

The assurance of His abiding love is of great comfort in all ways and during all of our days.

HOW DOES GOD LOVE?

The complete answer as to how God loves is hidden in the mysteries of the universe. However, we know that his very nature is love.

There is no way to exhaust His love. It is literally true as Bailey has said, *"Love spends his all, and still hath store."* The following words are reported to have been discovered on the walls of an ancient asylum. They beautifully speak of the Lord's inexhaustible love for you at all times.

Could we with ink the ocean fill,
And were the skies of parchment made,
Were every stalk on earth a quill,
And every man a scribe by trade.
To write the love, of God above,
Would drain the ocean dry.
Nor could the scroll, contain the whole,
Though stretched from sky to sky.

God's love is often revealed through others. He sends His healing on the wings of friends and loved ones.

"What stopped you from taking your own life?" This question I asked a school teacher who said she had planned to do so a few days before. Her answer, *"Because of one of my students."*

She went on to explain that the day she intended to take her life one of her pupils had come up and kissed her on the cheek. It was a spontaneous expression of love. The little girl uttered no words, but only kissed her teacher.

Depressed, dejected, and lonely there loomed before her eyes and heart the kiss of this little girl. It sustained her in her most desperate moment.

There are many through whom God shows His love to us each day. You are called to receive this love as well as to seek to impart love. His health care plan is carefully balanced. It is a balance of giving and receiving — receiving and giving. Both aspects must be present.

Love not only reaches in, but it reaches out as well. Markham put it succinctly when he wrote:

He drew a circle that shut me out —
Heretic, rebel, a thing to flout.
But love and I had the wit to win;
We drew a circle that took him in.

God's Health Care Plan - Joy

Joy is defined as, *"to be glad; rejoice; a lively emotion of happiness; gladness."*

Ardis Whitman speaks of joy as, *"Awe and a sense of mystery are part of it; so are the feelings of humility and gratitude. Suddenly we are keenly aware of every living thing — every leaf, every flower, every cloud, the mayfly hovering over the pond, the crow cawing in the treetops."*

There are many references to joy.

"A merry heart maketh a cheerful countenance; but by sorrow of the heart the spirit is broken." (Pro. 15:13)

"...he that is of a merry heart hath a continual feast." (Pro. 15:15)

A merry heart doeth good like medicine; but a broken spirit drieth the bones." (Pro. 17:22)

It is obvious from these verses that the disposition influences one's health condition. Also, we know that one's health condition influences disposition. You feel worse when you are disgruntled and sorrowful of heart. You feel better when you are full of joy. Joy does serve as a wonderful medicine.

WHERE DO YOU FIND JOY?

Joy cannot be contrived or falsely assumed. It is found in the very essence of life itself. The Giver of life and the One who is the Life is the Lord Himself. It is in His presence and because of His presence that we are able to have true joy.

"Thou wilt shew me the path of life: in thy presence is fullness of joy; at thy right hand there are pleasures for evermore." (Ps. 16:11)

Jesus was specific in saying that joy was His gift to all who believe in Him. *"These things have I spoken unto you, that my joy might remain in you, and that your joy might be full."* (John 15:11) *"And ye now therefore have sorrow; but I will see you again, and your heart shall rejoice, and your joy no man taketh from you."* (John 16:22)

DISCOVER JOY

Someone has said, *"The religion that makes a man look sick certainly won't cure the world."* Some believers act as if the world is the victor instead of the One whom they worship.

God's health care program certainly includes joy. There are some steps which will help you on your pilgrimage to and with joy.

1. *Realize your position in the Lord.* He has granted you the honor of being His child. He cares for you more than for all the material world.

2. *Develop the desire and ability to praise the Lord in all things and at all times.* This does not mean that you piously act as if all things were as the Lord wants them to be. This is not true. However, praise does acknowledge you believe the Lord is with you. He will see you through the darkest night and the deepest problem.

The *Dead Sea Scrolls* revealed great truth concerning praise as found in their *"Manual for Discipline."*

"As long as I live it shall be a rule engraved on my tongue to bring praise like fruit for an offering and my lips as a sacrificial gift.

"I will make skillful music with lyre and harp to serve God's glory, and the flute of my lips I raise in praise of His rule of righteousness. Both morning and evening I shall enter into the Covenant of God; and at the end of both I shall recite His commandments, and so long as they continue to exist, there will be my frontier and my journey's end.

"Therefore I will bless His name in all I do, before I move hand or foot, whenever I go out or come in, when I sit down and when I rise, even when lying on my couch, I will chant His praise. My lips shall praise Him as I sit at the table which is set for all, and before I lift my hand to partake of any nourishment from the delicious fruits of the earth. When fear and terror come, and there is only anguish and distress, I will still bless and thank Him for His wondrous deeds, and meditate upon His power, and lean upon His mercies all day long... So when trouble comes or salvation I praise Him just the same." See Phil 4:4.

God's Health Care Plan - Peace

God has designed His health care program to help you remain healthy. If you do become ill, His program will hasten recovery.

An important facet of His program is peace. He desires it for you. It is something the unbelieving and rebellious person does not have. *"There is no peace saith the Lord, unto the wicked."* (Isa. 48:22)

WHAT IS PEACE?

The dictionary defines personal peace as, *"a state of quiet or tranquility; freedom from disturbance or agitation; calm; repose; freedom from mental agitation or anxiety; spiritual contentment."* There is little doubt but that everyone wants this peace.

IMPORTANCE

Peace is so important to your wholeness. There can be no really whole life without it. Matthew Henry said, *"Peace is such a precious jewel that I would give anything for it but truth."* Jesus felt peace was so important that practically the last thing He said to His disciples was that they would receive His peace. *"My peace I leave with you, my peace I give unto you: not as the world giveth,..."* (John 16:33) Peace was the only estate He left them. He had no earthly possessions, but He had the most important possession. He wanted them to have it, too.

Many Scriptures speak of the importance of peace.

"...seek peace, and pursue it." (Ps. 34:14)

"...let peace rule in your hearts." (Col. 3:15)

OBSTACLES

There are many obstacles to personal peace. Many never overcome these obstacles. They seek peace more and more and find it less and less.

The biggest obstacle is the inner person. The real obstacles are not the tangible outward circumstances but the inward feelings. An ancient writer summarized obstacles to peace, *"Five great enemies to peace inhabit with us: vice, avarice, wicked ambition, envy, anger, and pride. If these enemies were to be banished, we should infallibly enjoy perpetual peace."*

Thus the disturber of peace and the preventer of peace is the spirit which permeates the inner person. Every spirit which is contrary to the spirit of the Lord will rob you of peace. Every action which is contrary to the moral and spiritual laws of the Lord contributes toward your continuing lack of peace.

GIVER OF PEACE

Peace is so desirable that practically everyone is searching for it. But what or who brings peace? Many are seeking it through artificial means. They are traveling under the illusion that they will be given peace through drugs, or sex, or the occult, or religious cults, or humanistic meditation or a combination of these. The ultimate end of such efforts is not peace, but more problems.

There are no peace pills available. Peace is a gift of the Lord. The Giver of the only peace which ultimately satisfies is Jesus. He says, *"My peace I give unto you."* See Eph. 2:14; Col. 1:20; Isa. 53:5.

STEPS TO PEACE

The road to peace leads directly to the Lord. The road to peace has the Lord as your traveling companion.

The following steps will get you started on the road of peace and will keep you on this road.

1. *Sincerely believe the Lord loves you and commit yourself to Him.* Eliphaz spoke eternal truth when he said, *"Acquaint now thyself with him, and be at peace..."* (Job 22:21) Paul was even more specific with, *"For Christ is our peace..."* (Eph. 2:14) Someone has said, *"There is but one way to tranquility of mind and happiness, and that is to account no external things thine own, but to commit all to God."*

2. *Search the Scriptures and obey their teachings.* The Psalmist declares, *"Great peace have they which love thy law: and nothing shall offend them."* (Ps. 119:165)

Reading, seeking to understand and to obey God's Word is a giant stride toward peace. I like Smiley Blanton's, Director of the American Foundation of Religion and Psychiatry, reply to the question of his reading the Bible.

"I not only read it, I study it. It's the greatest textbook on human behavior ever put together. If people would just absorb its message, a lot of us psychiatrists could close our offices and go fishing."

3. *Realize peace is a Person and not a place or a position.* I suggest that you picture yourself at the most beautiful and perfect spot you can imagine. Now, let the Lord Jesus enter into your life. Quiet your body, mind, and spirit. Absorb the peace of His presence. He will impart His peace during these moments. This peace is yours every moment. Claim His peace today! (I Cor. 1:3)

God's Health Care Plan - Patience

Patience is certainly a part of God's health care plan. It is included in His prescription for a full and healthy life.

The fruit of the Spirit as mentioned in Gal. 5:22 helps you to live a healthier life. The Lord wants you to be whole. He is not simply interested in healing you after you have become ill.

A skilled medical person told me that physicians are taught primarily to treat disease. They are not taught how to direct people to help them live and to maintain a healthy life. Their practice and efforts are primarily directed toward crises instead of preventive measures.

The greatest need in your life and mine is how to keep from becoming ill. Patience developed to its fullest will help a great deal.

WHAT IS PATIENCE?

The dictionary defines patience as, *"the exercise of sustained endurance and perserverance; the forbearance toward the faults or infirmities of others; tranquil waiting or expectation; ability to await events without perturbation. Patience is keeping kindliness of heart under vexatious conduct; long-suffering is continued patience. Patience may also have an active force denoting uncomplaining steadiness in doing.* Synonyms are: *calmness, composure, endurance, forbearance, fortitude, leniency, long-suffering, resignation, submission, and sufferance."*

FRUIT OF IMPATIENCE

Impatience spawns many problems. It leads to flared tempers, unproductive short-cuts to solve problems, and uneasiness and unhappiness with life. It will lead to your doubting the Lord. You will want things you are not receiving. Often your desired timing is not the Lord's timing and the result is a frustrated life for you.

A friend of Dr. Phillips Brooks observed him pacing the floor like a caged animal. *"What's the trouble?"* he asked. Dr. Brooks replied, *"Trouble, I'll tell you the trouble. I'm in a hurry and God isn't."* Isn't this often your problem? You want to have the quick easy answer to all situations. You want to lift your petitions to the Lord by noon, and have all the answers by sundown. However, the Lord's timetable is often different than yours. He will answer in His own time and in His own way.

There are many examples of impatience in the Bible. Consider: Moses when Israel murmured (Num. 20:10); Naaman at Elisha's suggestion (II Kings 5:11,12); Jonah at the short-lived gourd (Jonah 4:8,9); Disciples at the Syrophenician woman (Mt. 15:23); James and John at the Samaritans (Lu. 9:54); Martha at Mary (Lu. 10:40); and Abram and Sarai at birth of Ishmael (Gen. 16:1-6).

WAIT ON THE LORD

The life of patience and perseverance is one that waits upon the Lord. We are to wait upon the Lord. Many expect the Lord to wait upon them. The Psalmist wrote, *"Wait on the Lord, be of good courage, and he shall strengthen thine heart: wait I say, on the Lord."* (Ps. 31:24)

There is no way we can set the Lord's pace. We are to fit into His plans and thereby find the power and peace which can be ours.

STEPS TO PATIENCE

1. *Recall and remember how patient the Lord has been and continues to be with you.* Thank God for this truth, *"The Lord is merciful and gracious, slow to anger, and plenteous in mercy...For he knoweth our frame; he remembereth that we are dust."* (Ps. 103:8,14)

2. *Realize you are not called to be the judge or the one who imparts the punishment.* The Bible tells us God judges and metes out punishment. *"Dearly beloved, avenge not yourselves, but rather give place unto wrath; for it is written, Vengeance is mine, I will repay, saith the Lord."* (Rom. 12:19) See (Pro. 20:22)

3. *Be willing to suffer for the Lord and for righteousness sake.* You may be irritated by the actions and/or inaction of others. However, it is to the Lord that you must constantly look. *"For what glory is it, if, when ye be buffeted for your faults, ye shall take it patiently? But if, when ye do well, and suffer for it, ye take it patiently, this is acceptable with God. For even hereunto were ye called; because Christ also suffered for us, leaving us an example..."* (I Pet. 2:20,21)

4. *Realize that as you develop patience the Lord becomes more real to you and strengthens your inward being. He enables you to face all circumstances.* You are healthier and truly a participant in the Lord's health care plan. *"They that wait upon the Lord shall renew their strength..."* (Isa. 40:31)

God's Health Care Plan - Kindness

Partaking of the fruit of the spirit certainly enables an individual to be healthier. One of the most precious aspects of the fruit of the spirit is *kindness.*

Kindness is the gentle, tender, good deed which reaches out to others, while at the same time reaching deep within yourself. The Apostle Paul sums it up, *"Be kindly affectioned one to another with brotherly love; in honour preferring one another."* (Rom 12:10)

Kindness is not easily defined, but is easily felt and experienced. It encompasses more than can be readily verbalized. It is an act in the best interest of the one for whom it is done. It blesses the blessed and the blesser.

EACH DAY

You should seek to do at least one act of kindness each day. Kindness is a tangible step to overcoming the human tendency of selfishness. It is very much a part of God's health care plan. The selfish life is a sick life. The selfish soul is a stifled soul.

Bailey has said, *"Both man and womankind belie their nature when they are not kind."* Acts of kindness accent the higher nature of man. They release the power of the Lord in and through you.

Years ago an experiment was conducted concerning energy efficiency and the condition of the pavement. The electric trolley was tested on several different types of pavement. It was learned that 20% more power was needed to run at twelve miles an hour over a poor asphalt pavement than over a good one. It took 40% to 60% more power with a pavement in various stages of deterioration.

Is not this illustrative of our lives? Our meanness, injustices, and selfishness can make it very difficult for ourselves and others. On the other hand kindness can smooth out the road of life for others and ourselves. The wear and tear on an individual is a great deal less when kindness is the dominant aspect of life.

A STRAIGHT LINE

You should not expect a direct return of kindness from the one to whom you are kind. So often it just doesn't work that way. My wife's Grandma Bell always said, *"Acts of kindness travel in a straight line."* You pass on to another an act of kindness in response to the many you have received from others.

A young man returned from visiting a shut-in and expressed his good feeling. The shut-in will never be able to return his call. But through other channels I'm sure kindness will come to this young man.

A postman friend of mine beamed as he told how good it felt to tramp through the snow to secure a letter being mailed by an elderly man. Simple acts of kindness, yes; but what a difference they make in the life of the one conveying them and the ones to whom they are conveyed.

UNKINDNESS CANNOT DEFEAT

Please do not let an unkind act toward you defeat your reaching out in kindness. Nurturing a resentment or an unkindness can only lead to distress and disease.

God's health care plan calls for you to be kind in the face of any and all unkindness. Dr. Dan Poling was complaining about the hypocrites and spiritual leaders in his congregation. His good friend, Dr. Cadman, gave sage advice, *"I know, I know, but if you want to help them and save yourself, you'll have to learn to love them, my boy."*

An ounce of kindness is worth a ton of admonition. God's health care plan requires that we maintain a life of devotion to Him.

RECEIVE KINDNESS

One of the most difficult things for many of us is to graciously receive a kindness. We often feel so unworthy. May you never say no to a kindness with either words or actions. Simply receive the kindness as from the Lord, regardless of whom His channel may be. Thoreau said, *"It is something to be able to paint a particular picture, ...make a few objects beautiful; ...but it is far more glorious...to affect the quality of the day — that is the highest of arts."* See (Eph. 4:32)

God's Health Care Plan - Goodness

William Penn said, *"I expect to pass through life but once. If therefore, there be any kindness I can show, or any good I can do to any fellow-being, let me do it now, and not defer nor neglect it, as I shall not pass this way again."*

He placed an emphasis upon goodness which is true to Scripture and the principles of good health. Goodness is indeed part and parcel of God's health care plan. The ultimate end of neglecting goodness is alienation from the Lord, others, and oneself.

Walt Whitman certainly put the proper emphasis upon goodness when he wrote, *"Roaming in thought over the universe, I saw the little that is good steadily hastening towards immortality, and the vast that is evil I saw hastening to merge itself and become lost and dead."*

OUR GOODNESS

Most of us possess what I call an Archie Bunker type of goodness. That is, a bit of goodness and mercy among a lot of bigotry and prejudice and injustice.

Montaigne put it succinctly, *"There is no one so good, who, were he to submit all his thoughts and actions to the law, would not deserve hanging ten times in his life."*

God's health care plan calls for your life to be aimed at consistent goodness. The direction you walk affects the health of your body, soul, and spirit.

WHAT IS GOOD?

The dictionary definition of good is, *"having or characterized by admirable moral or spiritual qualities; especially, governed by dutiful regard for the moral and divine law, conformed to the law of right; righteous; virtuous, religious: opposed to bad, evil, vicious, wicked."*

I was amazed to discover the dictionary listed 75 synonyms for the word good. In fact, it finally gave up listing synonyms and summarized with, *"Good may at some time be a synonym of almost any adjective in the language implying advantage, benefit, utility, worth, etc."*

THE BIBLE AND GOODNESS

The Apostle Paul lists goodness as a characteristic of the fruit of the spirit. (Gal. 5:22) Dr. Wm. Barclay says that the word used for goodness in this verse is not found in secular Greek. It has a unique Biblical significance. He defines the Greek word translated goodness as, *"virtue equipped at every point."* It is a quality of life which can rebuke, correct, and discipline. It often presents problems for some as it runs counter to their concepts or conduct. For instance, Jesus sought to do good by cleansing the temple, but incurred the wrath of some in so doing.

Paul speaks of the brethren being filled with goodness (Rom. 15:14); quality of the fruit of the spirit (Eph. 5:9); and desired in the believer's life (II Th. 1:11). Consider: I Cor. 9:8; Gal. 6:10; Phil. 4:8; I Thes. 5:15,21)

BE GOOD FOR GOODNESS SAKE

There can be no fullness of the fruit of the spirit without goodness. Goodness is the measure of success far more than acquisition of things. A speaker was heralding the attractiveness of the advances of technology. He pointed out how it had brought so many better things to many people. One of the old timers sobered the thinking of all when he remarked, *"To be better off is not to be better."* Bishop Horne drives this point home with his insights, *"In the heraldry of heaven goodness precedes greatness, and so on earth it is more powerful. The lowly and lovely may often do more good in their limited sphere than the gifted."*

Make goodness a vital part of your health plans for goodness sake. *"...For he that...will see good days...let him...do good;"* (I Pet. 3:10,11)

God's Health Care Plan - Faithfulness

Faithfulness is a stirring word. It almost shouts its message of devotion, firmness, loyalty, truth, trustworthiness, and unwavering style of life. It is the respected way of living in the world and the required way in our relationships with God. The clarion call of scripture is to faithfulness. *"Be faithful unto death, and I will give you the crown of life."* (Rev. 2:10)

It is one thing to begin to follow the Lord and another to finish the race. Many start with great enthusiasm which quickly wanes and in some completely dies. There is nothing more heartbreaking than to counsel an individual in distress because of unfaithfulness to a spouse, business partner, neighbor, family member, etc. Their loyalty to the ways of the Lord has been compromised through their relationship with others. Jesus gave a call to faithfulness. *"No man having put his hand to the plough, and looking back, is fit for the kingdom of God."* (Lu. 9:62)

UNFAITHFULNESS

The health the Lord desires for you can be impaired and destroyed by acts of unfaithfulness toward the Lord and/or those around you. It can lead to mental and emotional illnesses which can ultimately affect you physically. The final fruit of unfaithfulness is not the sweet and nourishing fruit anticipated. Ultimately it is bitter fruit which is harvested from unfaithfulness.

What leads to unfaithfulness? What causes a person to get eyes off the real goal and to gaze upon lesser goals? Why does one step from the path of openness and light into the realm of unfaithfulness and darkness? Jesus gave three reasons for unfaithfulness and they can be applied to practically any area of life. He presents them through the parable of the sower. (Lu. 8:1-15)

1. *The devil* — The evil one immediately takes away the word of truth from the heart so you will not believe. Your desire for faithfulness is immediately ignored or suppressed.

2. *Temptation* — There are those who are determined to be faithful, but only continue this way for a short time. They yield to the temptation to take the easy way and choose short term benefits.

Frequently the temptations of the flesh are too much for them. It is intriguing to read in the book, *"Daughter of Destiny,"* that even some of Kathryn Kuhlman's coworkers succumbed to the passions of immorality and the love of money. Even Kathryn, as a young woman, could not resist the lure of the passions and married a divorced man. This act put her ministry in mothballs for nearly ten years and remained a blight on her efforts to the day of her death. The path of unfaithfulness is inviting. The end of the path is disappointment, heartache, and often mental, emotional, or physical illness.

3. *Life's attractions* — There are many who have been unable to resist the cares, riches, and pleasures of this life. Many a great and promising ministry has been devastated through unfaithfulness caused by a creeping love of riches, glory, and honor which crowds out loyalty, devotion, and submission to the Lord Jesus Christ. Unfaithfulness is not new to our day. Demas forsook Paul as did all others. (II Tim. 4:10,16)

YOU CAN BE FAITHFUL

It is possible to remain faithful to the Lord and to others. Faithfulness is a part of God's health care plan. Try these steps:

1. *Take the long look at your life and your present situation.* What is most wholesome is not always what is expedient.

2. *Keep close to and open to other believers.* The member of Alcoholics Anonymous is instructed to talk to another member when the moments of temptation come to return to the bottle. This is good advice for any area of temptation. Sharing with another person that you are going through moments of great temptation is to often receive the strength to remain faithful.

3. *Keep your eyes upon Jesus.* He is your salvation and strength. Unfaithfulness results when you look elsewhere for your joy, pleasure, etc. I recall a cartoon which dramatically presented the fundamentals of faithfulness. Pictured was a blazing sun in the heavens, a daffodil growing near a basement window, and a dim electric light bulb which could be seen through a dirty window. The daffodil was bent toward the dim light bulb and away from the glorious sun. The caption underneath was one word, *infidelity.* (I Co. 10:13)

God's Health Care Plan - Gentleness

"You are going to have to calm down, and learn to control your anger and keep relaxed." These are the words his physician spoke to a friend of mine who was recovering from a third heart attack. His turbulent spirit had and would continue to affect his heart. A more gentle spirit would determine not only the quality but the quantity of his years.

YOUR GENTLENESS

Your gentleness of spirit is certainly part of the Lord's plan for your overall health. The gentle spirit helps us to live a more abundant and healthful life.

The gentle individual is one who is mild of disposition and gracious in spirit. It is the spirit to which believers are called. *"And the servant of the Lord must not strive; but be gentle unto all..."* (II Tim. 2:24) *"To speak evil of no man, to be no brawlers, but gentle, showing all meekness unto all men."* (Tit. 3:2)

POWER OF GENTLENESS

Paul could be blunt and to the point. However, he still sought to minister in a spirit of gentleness. The gentle spirit affected not ony the health of the individual but the health of the church. Paul knew the power of gentleness. It was a great persuader in his eyes. *"Now I Paul myself beseech you by the meekness and gentleness of Christ..."* (II Cor. 10:1) *"But, we were gentle among you even as a nurse cherisheth her children."* (I Th. 2:7)

The fable concerning the north wind and the sun illustrates the power of gentleness. They had a contest to see which could most quickly get a man to remove his coat. The north wind made the first attempt and blew fiercely. The harder he blew the tighter the man drew his coat around him.

The sun took his turn and focused his gentle warmth upon the man. It was not long until the coat was loosened, then unbuttoned, and soon completely removed. The sun had accomplished by gentleness what the north wind could never do through harshness. The gentle spirit is ultimately the most powerful in our own lives and the lives of others.

PURSUE GENTLENESS

The following are some of the reasons you should seek to develop the spirit of gentleness.

1. The Lord Jesus reached out to others in a spirit of gentleness. *"Come unto me...for I am meek and lowly in heart:..."* (Mt. 11:28-30)

2. One of the qualities of the wisdom the Lord wants you to possess is gentleness. Consider: *"But the wisdom that is from above is first pure, then peaceable, gentle, and easy to be entreated...."* (James 3:17)

3. The mature and confident spirit is a gentle spirit. Fenelon has said, *"It is only imperfection that complains of what is imperfect. The more perfect we are, the more gentle and quiet we become toward the defect in others."*

Gentleness begets gentleness. Your health and the well being of others will be enhanced if you develop and maintain a spirit of gentleness.

How beautifully the following speaks to us.

"Go placidly amid the noise and haste, and remember what peace there may be in silence. As far as possible without surrender be on good terms with all persons. Speak your truth quietly and clearly; and listen to others, even the dull and ignorant; they too have their story.

"Avoid loud and aggressive persons, they are vexations to the spirit. If you compare yourself with others, you may become vain and bitter; for always there will be greater and lesser persons than yourself. Enjoy your achievements as well as your plans.

"Keep interested in your own career, however humble; it is a real possession in the changing fortunes of time. Exercise caution in your business affairs; for the world is full of trickery. But let this not blind you to what virtue there is; many persons strive for high ideals, and everywhere life is full of heroism.

"Be yourself. Especially, do not feign affection. Neither be cynical about love; for in the face of all aridity and disenchantment it is perennial as the grass.

"Take kindly the counsel of the years, gracefully surrendering the things of youth. Nurture strength of spirit to shield you in sudden misfortunes. But do not distress yourself with imaginings. Many fears are born of fatigue and loneliness. Beyond a wholesome discipline be gentle with yourself. You are a child of the universe, no less than the trees and the stars; you have a right to be here. And whether or not it is clear to you, no doubt the universe is unfolding as it should.

"Therefore be at peace with God, whatever you conceive Him to be, and whatever your labors and aspirations, in the noisy confusion of life keep peace with your soul.

"With all its sham, drudgery and broken dreams, it is still a beautiful world. Be careful. Strive to be happy." I pray the gentle spirit will be yours now and always.

God's Health Care Plan - Self Control

While taking his daily walk an ancient king was startled by the sudden appearance of an old bearded man. The surprised king blurted out, *"And who are you?"* The aged man's answer, *"I am a king,"* was even more startling than his sudden appearance. *"A king! Over what country do you reign?"* asked the amazed and amused monarch.

"Over myself. I rule myself because I control myself. I am my own subject to command," was the old man's humble but wise and honest answer.

CALL TO SELF-CONTROL

Self-control is part of the fruit of the spirit which issues forth in better health for all who practice it. It is part of God's health care plan. (Gal. 5:22) It is part of the life which is lived to the fullest. *"He that is slow to anger is better than the mighty; and he that ruleth his spirit than he that taketh a city."* (Pro. 16:32) See (Rom. 6:12,13; I Pet. 1:5,6)

LACKING

Much of my time is consumed counseling those who have not been able to practice self control. Also, frequently I see those who have been hurt by the uncontrolled actions of others.

The fruit of the lack of self-control is ultimately chaos. Lack of self-control manifests itself in strife, drunkenness, overweight, sexual immorality, dependence upon drugs, indifference to the feelings and needs of others, an extremely selfish view of life, etc. All of the above and their consequences lead to a life of defeat, remorse, frustration, depression, desperation, and spiritual bankruptcy.

CONTRIBUTES TO WHOLENESS

Self-control helps you to live the life which produces and maintains the wholeness the Lord desires for you. You, as a believer, practice self-control not because of the law which forbids; but because of God's love which frees.

Any worthwhile achievement requires self-control and discipline. The achiever is one who is willing to pay the price. Paul puts it well, *"And every man that striveth for the mastery is temperate in all things..."* (I Cor. 9:25)

Each believer should seek to practice self-control in all areas even more than does the athlete. *"...now they do it to obtain a corruptible crown; but we an incorruptible."* (I Cor. 9:25)

This does not mean that you must forsake life, but that you subdue the passions of life. There is a world of difference between legitimate pleasures being enjoyed and sensual passions being unbridled.

Aristippus said, *"The conqueror of pleasure is not the man who never uses pleasure. He is the man who uses pleasure as a ride guides a horse or a steersman directs a ship and so directs them wherever he wishes."*

PRACTICE SELF-CONTROL

It is much easier for me to present the problems resulting from lack of self-control than it is to give guidance for you to practice self-control. However, the following practical steps may be helpful:

1. *Center your life upon Jesus.* Make His goals your goals. He lived His life with eternal values in mind. You are called to do likewise. (Phil. 2:5) It is so easy to have your attention diverted to lesser goals and desires. The winner of the race of life is the one who looks to Jesus. (Heb. 12:1)

2. *Think upon the things which uplift and enhance.* I often say that evil thoughts permitted to stay will cause our actions soon to stray. (Phil. 4:8)

3. *Realize that self-control is determined to a large extent by how well you control your tongue.* Observe what James says, *"And the tongue is a fire, a world of iniquity; ...full of deadly poison."* (James 3:6-8)

If self-control of the tongue were practiced many of the ills of the world would be removed and controlled and even healed.

"The boneless tongue, so small, so weak
Can crush and kill," declares the Greek.
"The tongue destroys a greater horde,"
The Turks assert, *"than does the sword."*
The Persian proverb wisely saith;
"A lengthy tongue, an early death."
Or sometimes takes this form instead:
"The tongue can speak a word whose speed,"
Says the Chinese, *"outstrips the steed."*
While Arab sages this impart!
"The tongue's great storehouse is the heart."
From Hebrew writ this saying sprung:
"Tho' feet should slip, ne'er let the tongue."
The Sacred writers crown the whole:
"Who keeps his tongue doth keep his soul."

CONCLUSION

A wise person of by-gone ages said that life had four great principles. Self-control is one of them. His four great principles are:

"Wisdom, the principle of doing things aright; Justice, the principle of doing things equally in public and in private; Fortitude, the principle of not fleeing danger, but meeting it; and Temperance (self-control), the principle of subduing desires and living moderately."

God has a health care plan for you. Believe it! Practice it!

God's health care plan does include — love, joy, peace, patience, kindness, goodness, faithfulness, gentleness, and self-control. Follow His plan!

The Hands of Jesus

Hands fascinate me. They are miracles of perfection. They are versatile, powerful, beautiful. The hands serve worthy or unworthy purposes according to our desires. The heart determines if they will be used to cradle a child or to commit a murder.

We use our hands to greet a friend, feed ourselves, ward off an attacker, express approval or disapproval, wave good-bye, type a letter, change a tire, read Braille, and a thousand and one other things. The hand in and of itself is unaccountable for its actions and yet is involved in almost all of our overt acts.

PHYSICAL STRUCTURE

The 27 bones in the hand are more than 25% of the bones of the body. There are five bones in the palm, fourteen in the digits, and eight in the wrist. The average person will flex the fingers and make use of the hand over 25 million times in their life time.

One of the most unique aspects of the hand are the finger-tips. The finger prints appear in the fourth month of development and no two are alike. Everyone is a person in his/her own right as far as fingerprints are concerned.

These marvels of nature are enhanced further when you realize that two of the largest areas of the brain known as the motor cortex serve the hands.

HANDS AND HEALING

The Bible reveals to us the relationship of the hands and the release of the power of God. Jesus often touched and/or laid hands on individuals as He imparted wholeness to them.

THE HANDS OF JESUS

The hands of Jesus were instruments of help to many people. They were hands of labor, peace, blessing, sacrifice, hope, promise, power, and healing.

Jesus did not hesitate to use His hands to impart healing. Why should many in the church be so fearful of the ministry of laying-on-of-hands? Our insights and interpretation of the scriptures need to sharpen to the point of obedience in this area.

Please consider the following specific references to the touch of the Master's Hand. I hope you will be inspired and informed in so doing.

1. The leper — *"And Jesus put forth his hand, and touched him, saying, I will, be thou clean. And immediately his leprosy was cleansed."* (Mk. 1:41; Lu. 5:13)

2. The ruler's daughter — *"While he spake these things unto them, behold, there came a certain ruler, and worshipped him, saying, My daughter is even now dead: but come and lay hand upon her, and she shall live."* (Mt. 9:18; Mk. 5:23)

3. Peter's mother-in-law — *"And he touched her hand, and the fever left her: and she arose, and ministered unto them."* (Mt. 8:15; Mk. 1:31)

4. The deaf — *"And they bring unto him one that was deaf, and had an impediment in his speech; and they beseech him to put his hand upon him. And he took him aside from the multitude, and put his fingers into his ears, and he spit, and touched his tongue."* (Mk. 7:32,33)

5. The blind man — *"And he cometh to Bethsaida; and they bring a blind man unto him, and besought him to touch him. And he took the blind man by the hand, and led him out of the town; and when he had spit on his eyes, and put his hands upon him, he asked him if he saw ought. And he looked up, and said, I see men as trees, walking. After that he put his hands again upon his eyes, and made him look up: and he was restored, and saw every man clearly."* (Mk. 8:22-25)

6. The infirmity — *"And he laid hands on her; and immediately she was made straight, and glorified God."* (Lu. 13:13)

7. At Nazareth — *"And he could do no mighty work, save that he laid his hands upon a few sick folk, and healed them."* (Mk. 6:5)

8. The multitudes — *"Now when the sun was setting, all they that had any sick with divers diseases brought them unto him; and he laid his hands on every one of them, and healed them."* (Lu. 4:40)

Incidents 2, 4, and 5 are of special importance because Jesus was asked to lay-on-hands.

This request would not have been made if He had not been ministering in this fashion. They were requesting of the Master what they knew He did. They had seen Him lay on hands for the sick.

If Jesus practiced the laying-on-of-hands how can we as His followers neglect to do so?

Healed for Someone

The account of the healing of Peter's mother-in-law is recorded in Mt. 8:14-15; Mark 1:29-31; and Luke 4:38-39.

Jesus had visited the synagogue prior to this incident. He left from teaching about God to live out the power of God in His life.

Peter's family must have been one which was very close and very committed to the Lord. This was not a temporary thing, but lasted until the end.

Tradition tells us that Peter had to watch his wife tortured to death. Even while being tortured she rejoiced in the Lord. Peter was inspired by her example and as she breathed her last he called out to his faithful companion *"Remember thou the Lord."*

It was natural that Peter invite Jesus to his home. It was just as natural that Jesus ministered unto this devoted family.

FOR SOMEONE

Many when they are healed feel they are saved for something. They miss the point that they are healed for someone. Our wholeness is to be used for others and to the glory of God.

Peter's mother-in-law rose from the sick bed to minister unto others. She rejoiced in her healing, but more important she used her strength to minister unto others.

I would hope that all involved in the ministry of healing would remember that individuals are healed for Someone. That Someone is Jesus. He in turn wants the one healed to minister to others in His name.

I have seen many healed who then live a life contrary to the ways of the Lord. They almost live as if they were healed for continuing a selfish and rebellious life. Unless the heart is on the Lord the healed person will soon forget Who healed and why.

The writing of Oscar Wilde reveals so vividly that we must realize we are healed for Someone and not something. Otherwise a healing leads to or prolongs a life of continued disobedience and insignificance. Consider this vivid picture which he describes:

Christ came from a white plain to a purple city, and, as He passed through the first street, He heard voices overhead. He saw a young man lying drunk upon a window sill. *"Why do you waste your soul in drunkenness?"* The young man replied, *"Lord, I was a leper and you healed me. What else can I do?"*

A little farther through the town he saw a young man following a harlot. *"Why do you dissolve your soul in debauchery?"* The curt answer was, *"Lord, I was blind and you healed me, what else can I do?"*

In the middle of the city He saw an old man sitting on the ground and weeping. He asked, *"Why do you weep?"* The old man responded, *"Lord, I was dead and you raised me unto life. What else can I do but weep?"*

The three persons had missed the whole point of their marvelous healing. It was as if they were blaming the Lord instead of praising Him. They were continuing to center upon themselves instead of seeing they were healed for Christ and others. They had their heart on something instead of on Someone.

HOW SERVE

Why do you want to be healed? What will you do if you are healed? Where is your heart now and where will it be after your healing?

I hope you will answer that you want to be healed for Someone. You want to do His will. What can guide you in the doing of His will?

1. After you are healed do the task(s) at hand. Do the things and minister to the people in a way which uses the talents God has given you. Peter's mother-in-law rose from her sick bed and did what she could do best. She helped prepare the meal.

I often have individuals tell me they want to really serve the Lord. They want to do something great. They hope God will part the heavens and shout a message to them. They fail to see that they will serve best by doing what they have the talent to do. They serve best when they do the task which is at hand.

2. After you are healed let the wonder of His miracle power be seen through your service to others in His name.

Many are willing to tell of their miracle through a verbal testimony. This has its place, but the greatest testimony is service. Paul was delivered from the bite of the deadly serpent. He did not give his time to traveling and speaking of this miracle. No! He simply continued to serve the Lord. He had a task to do and he did it. He realized he was healed for Someone and not for something.

The Greatest Commission

I am often asked, *"Why do you put so much emphasis upon healing?" "Why are you so committed to the healing ministry?"*

My response is that I am not committed to the healing ministry. I am not committed to any ministry. I am committed to a person, Jesus Christ.

THE GREAT COMMISSION

Jesus gave to His Church the Greatest Commission.

> *"Go ye therefore, and teach all nations baptizing them in the name of the Father, and of the Son, and of the Holy Ghost."* Mt. 28:19

The question I raise is *"What shall His Church teach?" "What should be the heart of this message?"*

Why didn't Jesus specify at the end of His ministry what His followers were to teach? I feel it is because He had already thoroughly instructed them as to what they should teach and preach.

THE GREATEST COMMISSION

I feel you should teach what is found in what I call *"The Greatest Commission,"* which is given in Mt. 10:7,8 and Lu. 10:9.

THE TWELVE

Mt. 10:7,8 describes Jesus commissioning His twelve disciples. There is no doubt as to what He would have them to do. The message of healing is definitely part of what should be taught by His loyal followers. Jesus did not hedge in this area at all.

THE SEVENTY

Luke 10:9 records our Lord's words to seventy of His disciples.

> *"And heal the sick that are therein, and say unto them, the kingdom of God is come nigh unto you."*

Here again Jesus is very specific as to what His followers should be teaching and doing. There is no doubt, but what the Good News His followers were proclaiming included healing of the body, mind and spirit.

OBEDIENT

Thus, the Greatest Commission tells us exactly what we are to proclaim. It has specified what we are to teach. The content and emphasis of the commission is not omitted, hidden, or obscured. It is simply to take the message of wholeness to the world. The world needs this Good News. In a clear and concise manner Jesus commissioned His followers to see that the world receives it.

The message of healing is not an adjunct to the message of Good News. It is the message of Good News. Wholeness is salvation and salvation is wholeness. It is healing of the body, soul, and spirit which is to be heralded by the obedient followers of the Lord. It is the message the world needs to hear, must hear, and can hear through the ones completely obedient to the commission of the Master.

THE KINGDOM OF GOD

Jesus certainly felt that preaching and teaching the kingdom of God was a must for Him.

> *"I must preach the kingdom of God to other cities also, for therefore I am sent."* Mk. 1:38; Lu. 4:43

To this day we can proclaim that the kingdom of God is at hand. What better news can we proclaim?

The kingdom is not confined to the days of the Patriarchs or to the Apostolic age. The Kingdom is now. It is within you. (Lu. 17:21)

Jesus realized the fullness of the kingdom lay in the future. In His model prayer he instructed us to pray, *"Thy kingdom come."* (Mt. 6:10) But even as it is coming, it is here.

THE REAL QUESTION

The real basic question is not why do you proclaim healing. I feel the most basic is, how can you proclaim the Good News and omit the message of healing? The message of wholeness has never been rescinded. Who then is distorting the message of the Gospel? I feel it is the one who neglects to bring the Good News of wholeness to the *"sheep without a shepherd."*

Twice in the Gospels the Greatest Commission is given by our Lord. Thus, twice we are specifically told what to teach and what to proclaim. How many times do we have to be told before we are willing to do it?

Responsible for Receiving

There is no doubt about the fact that Jesus sent His disciples forth to heal the sick. He not only told them to go, but they went.

Jesus never tolerated a *"take it or leave it"* attitude on the part of those who heard His disciples proclaim the message of healing and hope. He placed heavy responsibility upon all who heard this message.

Please carefully and prayerfully consider the following words of our Lord Jesus:

To the twelve disciples:

> *"And whosoever shall not receive you...it shall be more tolerable for the land of Sodom and Gomorrah in the day of judgment, than for that city."* (Matthew 10:14,15)

To the seventy disciples:

> *"But into whatsoever city ye enter, and they receive you not, ...I say unto you, that it shall be more tolerable in that day for Sodom, than for that city."* (Luke 10:8,12)

Frequently believers interpret the above verses in the light of eternal salvation. Jesus was not talking about eternal life in these chapters. I know He told the seventy to rejoice that their names are written in heaven. This is wonderful. However, He first said unto them,

> *"Behold, I give unto you power to tread on serpents and scorpions, and over all the power of the enemy: and nothing shall by any means hurt you."* (Luke 10:19)

The gift of eternal life is no substitute for power in the life of a believer. It is no excuse to neglect the message of healing and hope.

Jesus spoke of harsh judgment being brought upon those who refuse the message of healing proclaimed by His disciples.

If you have been hesitant about the message of healing for our day you should carefully study Matthew 10 and Luke 10. They do not leave any loopholes for evasion of the message that Christ is the Great Physician.

You should keep the following truths in mind:

1. You as a believer are expected to believe Jesus and to receive and exercise His power in your life.
2. Those to whom you bring the message of healing will be held accountable for receiving this message.
3. The church proclaiming the message of healing should not be the exception, but should be the norm.
4. You are called to enlist others to help take out the message of healing to a sick and dying world.
5. There is an urgency to the Lord's message of wholeness. A ho-hum attitude will not be tolerated by Him. He expects obedience now and always. He is Lord, He is LORD.

Your Life Speaks

Have you ever heard the expression, *"Your actions speak so loud I cannot hear a word you say?"*

There is much truth in this statement. It is your life which speaks the loudest concerning your basic concepts and commitment. It is your lifestyle which reveals what you really believe.

It would be difficult to believe the words of a person proclaiming their devotion to the sacredness of life if they made their livelihood from child pornography.

It appears to be hypocrisy when a person speaks of the importance of the church and their love for it and they never attend nor support it in any way. Their actions speak much louder than their words.

It is difficult to hear mothers say they love their children and yet have them forsake them as they seek life with another mate or to live as a single. Actions speak louder than any number of words.

In like manner, what Jesus did is more important than what He said. His words are of utmost importance, but His deeds are even more important. He points this out,

> *"But I have greater witness than that of John: for the works which the Father hath given me to finish, the same works that I do, bear witness of me, that the Father hath sent me."* (John 5:36)

In a sense, John had only words. He certainly did not have the *"works"* of the Lord Jesus. He did not do miracles and healings as did Jesus.

There are many who are most willing to accept the teachings of Jesus. Many of these comprise what we call the Sermon on the Mount. (Matthew 5,6,7) I do not deny the depth and challenge of His teachings. They are important and they are essential. However, His lifestyle speaks louder than His words.

It is obvious from the gospels that His lifestyle was one of bringing wholeness to those unto whom He ministered. He brought to all a message of healing and of hope.

Prior to the Sermon on the Mount we have an account of the lifestyle of our Lord Jesus.

> *"And Jesus went about all Galilee, teaching...preaching...and healing all manner of sickness and all manner of disease among the people. And His fame went throughout all Syria: ...there followed Him great multitudes of people...."* (Mt. 4:23-25)

Following the Sermon on the Mount we have many incidents which depict the lifestyle of our Lord. They all bare witness of His desire and ability to bring wholeness unto those whom He met.

> *"...great multitudes followed Him...there came a leper...And Jesus put forth his hand, and touched him, saying, I will; be thou clean."* (Mt. 8:1-4)

There follows an account of miracle after miracle. I would suggest you read at this time Matthew 8:1 through Matthew 12:30.

It is indeed a mystery to me why so many are willing to accept His teaching but refuse His lifestyle. I do not infer we should neglect His teachings, but is not the lifestyle more important? Should we not seek to do what He did as well as to study what He said? Jesus put a lot of emphasis upon His lifestyle,

> *"If I do not the works of my Father, believe me not. But if I do, though ye believe not me, believe the works: ..."* (John 10:37,38)

The Healing Community

I conclude this book with a more lengthy article, because it is so important for you to realize you are not alone. Others are also a vital part of your pilgrimage to wholeness.

Many individuals believe they cannot be healed or that they cannot have a meaningful healing ministry because of their lack of faith. Your faith is important. I do not want to minimize this fact. However, your individual faith is not the determining factor as far as your healing is concerned. Your effective ministry of healing is not dependent upon your personal faith.

HEALING IS COMMUNITY

Healing is community. Healing is not something which takes place apart from others. The body of believers is the source of healing as the power of the Lord flows in and through the body. Our Lord Jesus has chosen to work through a body of believers and not to deposit His power in an individual.

True, there are some outstanding examples of individuals with great faith, great spiritual acumen, and great spiritual power. However, just as there may be one super player on a football team it still takes 10 other players to win the game. Thus, in the area of healing there may be some more prominent than others, but there are none who can go it alone.

THEIR FAITH

Jesus powerfully teaches that healing is community when he healed the paralytic. The incident is recorded in Matthew 9:1-8; Mark 2:1-12; Luke 5:17-26. The community of believers concept is evident when their author says, *"when Jesus saw* **their** *faith,"* Jesus said your sins are forgiven. A few moments later He said, *"take up your bed and walk."*

To whom does the word, *"their"* refer? We do not know. The only thing we know is that it means more than one person. It is plural. I do not know which ones of the five had faith. Did the four friends talk the sick man into coming to Jesus? Did the sick man and one or two of his friends persuade the others to carry him to Jesus? Did all five of them believe healing would come if they could get to Jesus? The answer is not given to these questions. The only thing we know for sure is that Jesus was impressed by the faith of more than one person. He honored the faith of a community of believers.

YOU DON'T GO IT ALONE

Isn't it refreshing and exciting to know that your healing and the healing ministry is not completely dependent upon you? There are others whose faith is blended with yours to make possible the victories in Jesus. Corporate faith is stronger than individual faith, just as a rope is many times stronger than any one of the strands of the rope.

I meet so many who feel they must go it alone. They fail to appreciate the fact that the Lord has provided others who also believe. They remind me of the famous organist who had come to town to present a Bach concert. The auditorium was packed and after a colorful and glowing introduction the organist announced, *"I am going to play Bach like you never heard Bach played before."*

He enthusiastically addressed himself to the keyboard. There was not a single sound. He tried again, but with no success. Flustered beyond words he frantically motioned to the gentleman pumping the billows to apply himself. The man just stood there looking up at the famous organist. After what seemed an eternity a loud whisper revealed the truth of community. The man at the billows whispered, *"Tell them* **we** *are going to play Bach like you have never heard Bach played before."*

We do not have the billows pumped by an individual today for the organ recital. However, can you imagine what would happen at a Virgil Fox concert if the workers at the electric plant refused to do their job? We live, work, believe in community. We must never forget this truth.

HOW MUCH FAITH DO I NEED

It is difficult to measure faith. Thank God we are not called to be measurers or evaluators of faith. We are called to be examples of faith. We are called to live by faith and not to develop a faith calculator to determine how much we have. Even a little faith, blended with others can accomplish a great deal.

The keeper of the lighthouse lighted a small candle and started up the stairs. The candle timidly said to him, *"Why do you do this? I am so small that my light can never be seen by ships in peril."* The master replied, *"No, but you will lighten my way to the top of the stairs."* In addition, when he had ascended the

stairs he used the small candle to light the huge beacon light which could be seen for miles. A little had accomplished much.

Remember that a large bank does not have millions of dollars because of one huge account. They have millions and millions of dollars because of thousands and thousands of accounts.

BLEND YOUR FAITH WITH OTHERS

You will be amazed at what will happen in your life and the life of your church, if you get your eyes off of worrying about your faith and trust the Lord along with others.

He will honor the corporate faith. When your faith is weak someone else's will be strong. When others may have weak faith yours will be strong. The community of believers is the way of the Lord as He imparts His wholeness.

A legend tells of a person granted a tour of the universe. He beheld a long table loaded with delicious food. However, the people seated at the table looked frail and alarmingly hungry. He then noticed that the utensils with which they were required to eat were so long that they could not get any food to their mouths. This banquet room was designated, Hell.

Soon he saw a similar banquet table spread with the bounties of mother earth. Those seated at the table were happy, looked well nourished, and were enjoying the meal. It was evident that the utensils were the same length. It was then that he noticed that each was feeding a friend across the table. What could not be done if you sought to feed yourself, could easily be accomplished for all if you fed another person. This banquet room was designated, Heaven.

May you reach out to others with your faith and let others reach out to you with theirs. Blend your faith with others and accept God's plan for wholeness and acknowledge that it is the community of believers from whence cometh the power of the Lord.

CONCLUSION

In conclusion, may I call to your attention that Jesus chose a community of twelve. He taught that where two or three are gathered — that is, community. The early church said, *"if any be sick let him call for the elders."* It was more than one elder. The healing ministry is not a hermit ministry. It is not confined to one. It is all of us together. It is all of us in and through Jesus Christ the Great Physician. Amen.

Healing RESOURCES for Clergy and Lay Persons

Qty.		Price	Total
______	ADVENTURES OF HEALING - Perhaps the most complete book available concerning healing. A gold mine of practical, easy to understand, yet biblical guidelines to an effective healing ministry. Jim Brown, a retired Presbyterian pastor, sums this book up best: "*. . . your book . . . is the most sane and sensible and Biblical . . . I've ever read. Thank you for it. If it were taken seriously, it would clear up a thousand misconceptions and help restore the healing ministry of our Lord to the total congregation and its responsibility to 'heal the sick and preach the gospel.'*"	12.95	______
______	MINISTRY OF THE MASTER - A daily devotional book with a difference. It presents a teaching about healing each day. Also, there is a joke each day and a Bible study for each week's theme. This devotional is a must for anyone who desires to come to a full understanding of the message and ministry of healing. Here is 440 pages concerning the lifestyle of our Lord Jesus Christ, which was bringing wholeness to those He met.	9.95	______
______	A MINISTRY OF PRAYER — (plus devotional cassette) - A guide to a thirty-day prayer pilgrimage. Groups and individuals have used this program to revolutionize their prayer life. Many churches have taken several groups through this pilgrimage. "*An excellent tool for understanding about prayer. It is a super pilgrimage. I gained so much personally from the experience. As a pastor, one of the thrilling things about this pilgrimage is that it can be led by a lay person. The format is so logical and the steps for implementation so easy to follow. I recommend it to one and all.*" Jay Schmidt, Pastor, Grace United Church of Christ, Canton, Ohio.	10.00	______
______	SPIRITUAL HEALING SEMINAR (6 - 60 min. cassettes) - Answers many of the most asked questions about healing. Each message is prepared for individual or group use. Lectures include: What is Spiritual Healing; Paul's Thorn In The Flesh; The Ministry of Laying-On-Of-Hands; Medicine and Spiritual Healing; The Weakness of Medicine; Why Anoint With Oil; Prayer and Spiritual Healing; What About Failures?; According To God's Will. A special bonus cassette includes Pastor Bartow's personal testimonial and examples of modern healings.	25.00	______
______	INNER HEALING (4 - 60 min. cassettes) - One of the most popular series by Pastor Bartow. He presents eight lectures with two major goals in mind: First, to bring inner healing to the one who listens; and, second, to present tangible and helpful guidance to anyone desiring to minister to those with inner illness. Discussed are major causes of inner illness and why it is the great epidemic of our day. Includes workable steps as to how one can receive inner healing. The prayer for inner healing presented in this series is worth the price of the set. This series should be required listening for any and all who realize the Lord's desire for wholeness and that He is willing to heal today.	20.00	______
______	A MINISTRY OF HEALING (8 - 60 Min. cassettes) - Hundreds have been helped through these lectures by Pastor Bartow. They have been recorded at the latest healing conference at Westminster Church and consider topics such as: Why a Ministry of Healing; Starting A Healing Ministry; Overcoming Obstacles to a Healing Ministry; How to conduct a Healing Service. This is the series for anyone interested in establishing a healing ministry.	40.00	______
		Sub-total	______
	Ohio residents add 5% sales tax.	Tax	______
		Total Enclosed	______

☐ Please send information about the Healing Conferences.

Name ________________________________

Church (As Applicable) ________________________________

Address ________________________________

City/State/Zip ________________________________

Life Enrichment Publishers • Box 526 H • Canton, Ohio 44701 • (216) 454-1598

Spiritual Healing Lay Leadership

WHAT - There are many lay persons who have been trained by Pastor Bartow to teach concerning the ministry of healing. They are most willing to help with a conference, seminar, or speak at worship, Sunday School, Bible Study or Prayer Groups.

COST - The cost involved is travel and lodging accomodations. The leaders are most willing to stay in a home whenever possible and preferred by the host church or group.

In addition, each church or group is asked to make a contribution for the Spiritual Healing Ministry. This may be an amount designated prior to the event or may be a free will offering at the time of the event.

The lay leaders receive no remuneration whatsoever.

LENGTH OF THE EVENT - This varies with the needs and desires of each church and/or group. It may be for only one service or may be for a day, several days, or a week-end. You set the pace and the lay leadership will adapt to it.

GUIDANCE - Once we receive your request further guidance will be given to you to make your experience most fruitful and helpful.

TEACHING - The lay leaders are capable of teaching and leading in the area of healing. In addition, video-cassettes by Pastor Bartow are available. They bring these video-cassettes with them and they are used for the presentations, if desired, and the lay leaders handle the question and answer periods, the healing services, etc.

REQUEST FORM

We desire to have lay leaders come to our community.

Name______________________________ Phone__________________

Church or group ____________________________________

Address ____

City/State/Zip _____________________________________

Nature of the event for which you desire lay leadership:__________________

____

____

Date: List your First choice ____________________ Second choice ____________________

What is the size of your church or group?______________ How many do you estimate will attend this event?______________

Will you seek to involve the community in this experience?____________________________

Send your request to: **The Spiritual Healing Ministry**
Box 92 Canton, Ohio 44701
Or phone: (216) 454-1598